Publishing

Decision Trees
for Business
Intelligence
and Data Mining

Using SAS® Enterprise Miner™

Barry de Ville

D1716267

The correct bibliographic citation for this manual is as follows: deVille, Barry. 2006. *Decision Trees for Business Intelligence and Data Mining: Using SAS® Enterprise Miner™*. Cary, NC: SAS Institute Inc.

Decision Trees for Business Intelligence and Data Mining: Using SAS® Enterprise Miner™

Contents

Preface:
Why Decision Trees?

Data has an important and unique role to play in modern civilization: in addition to its historic role as the raw material of the scientific method, it has gained increasing recognition as a key ingredient of modern industrial and business engineering. Our reliance on data—and the role that it can play in the discovery and confirmation of science, engineering, business, and social knowledge in a range of areas—is central to our view of the world as we know it.

Many techniques have evolved to consume data as raw material in the service of producing information and knowledge, often to confirm our hunches about how things work and to create new ways of doing things. Recently, many of these discovery techniques have been assembled into the general approaches of business intelligence and data mining.

Business intelligence provides a process and a framework to place data display and data analysis capabilities in the hands of frontline business users and business analysts. Data mining is a more specialized field of practice that uses a variety of computer-mediated tools and techniques to extract trends, patterns, and relationships from data. These trends, patterns, and relationships are often more subtle or complex than the relationships that are normally presented in a business intelligence context. Consequently, business intelligence and data mining are highly complementary approaches to exposing the full range of information and knowledge that is contained in data.

Some data mining techniques trace their roots to the origins of the scientific method and such statistical techniques as hypothesis testing and linear regression. Other techniques, such as neural networks, emerged out of relatively recent investigations in cognitive science: how does the human brain work? Can we reengineer its principles of operation as a software program? Other techniques, such as cluster analysis, evolved out of a range of disciplines rooted in the frameworks of scientific discovery and engineering power and practicality.

Decision trees are a class of data mining techniques that have roots in traditional statistical disciplines such as linear regression. Decision trees also share roots in the same field of cognitive science that produced neural networks. The earliest decision trees were modeled after biological processes (Belson 1956); others tried to mimic human methods of pattern detection and concept formation (Hunt, Marin, and Stone 1966).

As decision trees evolved, they turned out to have many useful features, both in the traditional fields of science and engineering and in a range of applied areas, including business intelligence and data mining. These useful features include:

- Decision trees produce results that communicate very well in symbolic and visual terms. Decision trees are easy to produce, easy to understand, and easy to use. One useful feature is the ability to incorporate multiple predictors in a simple, step-by-step fashion. The ability to incrementally build highly complex rule sets (which are built on simple, single association rules) is both simple and powerful.

- Decision trees readily incorporate various levels of measurement, including qualitative (e.g., good – bad) and quantitative measurements. Quantitative measurements include ordinal (e.g., high, medium, low categories) and interval (e.g., income, weight ranges) levels of measurement.

- Decision trees readily adapt to various twists and turns in data—unbalanced effects, nested effects, offsetting effects, interactions and nonlinearities—that frequently defeat other one-way and multi-way statistical and numeric approaches.

- Decision trees are nonparametric and highly robust (for example, they readily accommodate the incorporation of missing values) and produce similar effects regardless of the level of measurement of the fields that are used to construct decision tree branches (for example, a decision tree of income distribution will reveal similar results regardless of whether income is measured in 000s, in 10s of thousands, or even as a discrete range of values from 1 to 5).

To this day, decision trees continue to share inputs and influences from both statistical and cognitive science disciplines. And, just as science often paves the way to the application of results in engineering, so, too, have decision trees evolved to support the application of knowledge in a wide variety of applied areas such as marketing, sales, and quality control. This hybrid past and present can make decision trees interesting and useful to some, and frustrating to use and understand by others. The goal of this book is to increase the utility and decrease the futility of using decision trees.

This book talks about decision trees in business intelligence, data mining, business analytics, prediction, and knowledge discovery. It explains and illustrates the use of decision trees in data mining tasks and how these techniques complement and supplement other business intelligence applications, such as dimensional cubes (also called OLAP cubes) and data mining approaches, such as regression, cluster analysis, and neural networks.

SAS Enterprise Miner decision trees incorporate a range of useful techniques that have emerged from the various influences, which makes the most useful and powerful aspects of decision trees readily available. The operation and underlying concepts of these various influences are discussed in this book so that more people can benefit from them.

Acknowledgments

When I first started working with decision trees it was a relatively small and geographically dispersed community of practitioners. The knowledge that I have and the information that I communicate here is an amalgam of the graciously and often enthusiastically shared wisdom from this community – coaches, mentors, coworkers and advisors. While I am the scribe, in many ways it is *their* information that is being communicated. They include: Rolf Schliewen, Ed Suen, David Biggs, Barrie Bresnahan, Donald Michie, Dean MacKenzie, and Padraic Neville. I learned a lot about decision trees from many students while teaching courses internationally under the sponsorship of John Mangold and Ken Ono.

Padraic Neville and Pei-Yi Tan, SAS Enterprise Miner developers, coaxed me into putting this material together and kept adding fuel to ensure its completion. Padraic, in particular, took a lot of time out of his busy schedule to help launch this book and review the early drafts.

Julie Platt and John West from SAS Press were early supporters of the project and served as a constant and steady source of assistance and inspiration. This work would not have been completed without the perseverance and steady encouragement from this core team of supporters at SAS Institute.

The course notes on decision trees prepared by Will Potts, Bob Lucas, and Lorne Rothman in the Education Division at SAS were exceptionally useful and helped me clarify many of my thoughts. Wayne Donenfeld provided wide and deep review tasks that helped refine and clarify the content. I'd also like to thank the following reviewers at SAS: Brent Cohen, Leonardo Auslender, Lorne Rothman, Sascha Schubert, Craig DeVault, Dan Kelly, and Ross Bettinger.

Thank you all.

Decision Trees—
What Are They?

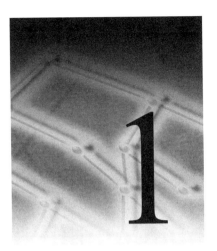

Introduction

Decision trees are a simple, but powerful form of multiple variable analysis. They provide unique capabilities to supplement, complement, and substitute for

- traditional statistical forms of analysis (such as multiple linear regression)
- a variety of data mining tools and techniques (such as neural networks)
- recently developed multidimensional forms of reporting and analysis found in the field of business intelligence

Decision trees are produced by algorithms that identify various ways of splitting a data set into branch-like segments. These segments form an inverted decision tree that originates with a root node at the top of the tree. The object of analysis is reflected in this root node as a simple, one-dimensional display in the decision tree interface. The name of the field of data that is the object of analysis is usually displayed, along with the spread or distribution of the values that are contained in that field. A sample decision tree is illustrated in Figure 1.1, which shows that the decision tree can reflect both a continuous and categorical object of analysis. The display of this node reflects all the data set records, fields, and field values that are found in the object of analysis. The discovery of the decision rule to form the branches or segments underneath the root node is based on a method that extracts the relationship between the object of analysis (that serves as the target field in the data) and one or more fields that serve as input fields to create the branches or segments. The values in the input field are used to estimate the likely value in the target field. The target field is also called an outcome, response, or dependent field or variable.

The general form of this modeling approach is illustrated in Figure 1.1. Once the relationship is extracted, then one or more decision rules can be derived that describe the relationships between inputs and targets. Rules can be selected and used to display the decision tree, which provides a means to visually examine and describe the tree-like network of relationships that characterize the input and target values. Decision rules can predict the values of new or unseen observations that contain values for the inputs, but might not contain values for the targets.

Figure 1.1: Illustration of the Decision Tree

Root Node
Display Total Data Set Value
of Target Field of Data

Input Field Used as Splitting Criterion

Field Value <1>
Field Value <2>
⋮
Field Value <n>

Field Value <n+1>
Field Value <n+2>
⋮
Field Value <N>

Node or leaf (bottom
nodes as shown here
are leaves)

Branch or Segment
Formed by Splitting
Rule

IF Input Field Value < n
THEN Target = Y%

IF Input Field Value > n
THEN Target = X%

Each rule assigns a record or observation from the data set to a node in a branch or segment based on the value of one of the fields or columns in the data set.[1] Fields or columns that are used to create the rule are called *inputs*. Splitting rules are applied one after another, resulting in a hierarchy of branches within branches that produces the characteristic inverted decision tree form. The nested hierarchy of branches is called a

[1] The SAS Enterprise Miner decision tree contains a variety of algorithms to handle missing values, including a unique algorithm to assign partial records to different segments when the value in the field that is being used to determine the segment is missing.

decision tree, and each segment or branch is called a *node*. A node with all its descendent segments forms an additional segment or a branch of that node. The bottom nodes of the decision tree are called *leaves* (or *terminal nodes*). For each leaf, the decision rule provides a unique path for data to enter the class that is defined as the leaf. All nodes, including the bottom leaf nodes, have mutually exclusive assignment rules; as a result, records or observations from the parent data set can be found in one node only. Once the decision rules have been determined, it is possible to use the rules to predict new node values based on new or unseen data. In predictive modeling, the decision rule yields the predicted value.

Figure 1.2: Illustration of Decision Tree Nomenclature

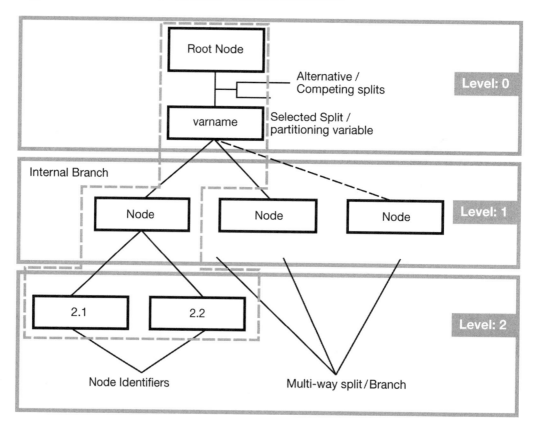

Although decision trees have been in development and use for over 50 years (one of the earliest uses of decision trees was in the study of television broadcasting by Belson in 1956), many new forms of decision trees are evolving that promise to provide exciting new capabilities in the areas of data mining and machine learning in the years to come. For example, one new form of the decision tree involves the creation of *random forests*. Random forests are multi-tree committees that use randomly drawn samples of data and inputs and reweighting techniques to develop multiple trees that, when combined, provide for stronger prediction and better diagnostics on the structure of the decision tree.

Besides modeling, decision trees can be used to explore and clarify data for dimensional cubes that can be found in business analytics and business intelligence.

Using Decision Trees with Other Modeling Approaches

Decision trees play well with other modeling approaches, such as regression, and can be used to select inputs or to create dummy variables representing interaction effects for regression equations. For example, Neville (1998) explains how to use decision trees to create stratified regression models by selecting different slices of the data population for in-depth regression modeling.

The essential idea in stratified regression is to recognize that the relationships in the data are not readily fitted for a constant, linear regression equation. As illustrated in Figure 1.3, a boundary in the data could suggest a partitioning so that different regression models of different forms can be more readily fitted in the strata that are formed by establishing this boundary. As Neville (1998) states, decision trees are well suited in identifying regression strata.

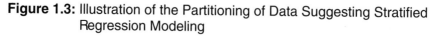

Figure 1.3: Illustration of the Partitioning of Data Suggesting Stratified Regression Modeling

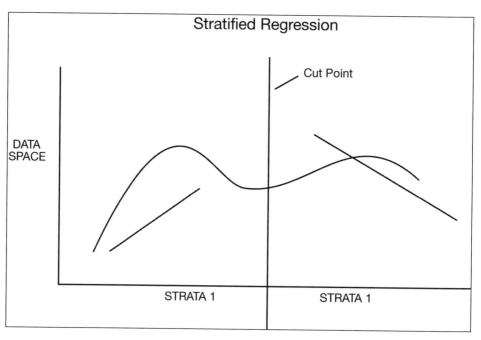

Decision trees are also useful for collapsing a set of categorical values into ranges that are aligned with the values of a selected target variable or value. This is sometimes called *optimal collapsing of values*. A typical way of collapsing categorical values together would be to join adjacent categories together. In this way 10 separate categories can be reduced to 5. In some cases, as illustrated in Figure 1.4, this results in a significant reduction in information. Here categories 1 and 2 are associated with extremely low and extremely high levels of the target value. In this example, the collapsed categories 3 and 4, 5 and 6, 7 and 8, and 9 and 10 work better in this type of deterministic collapsing framework; however, the anomalous outcome produced by collapsing categories 1 and 2 together should serve as a strong caution against adopting any such scheme on a regular basis.

Decision trees produce superior results. The dotted lines show how collapsing the categories with respect to the levels of the target yields different and better results. If we impose a monotonic restriction on the collapsing of categories—as we do when we request tree growth on the basis of ordinal predictors—then we see that category 1 becomes a group of its own. Categories 2, 3, and 4 join together and point to a relatively high level in the target. Categories 5, 6, and 7 join together to predict the lowest level of the target. And categories 8, 9, and 10 form the final group.

If a completely unordered grouping of the categorical codes is requested—as would be the case if the input was defined as "nominal"—then the 3 bins as shown in the bottom of Figure 1.4 might be produced. Here the categories 1, 5, 6, 7, 9, and 10 group together as associated with the highest level of the target. The medium target levels produce a grouping of categories 3, 4, and 8. The lone high target level that is associated with category 2 falls out as a category of its own.

Figure 1.4: Illustration of Forming Nodes by Binning Input-Target Relationships

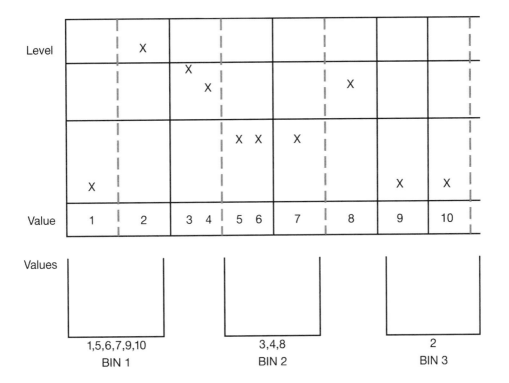

Since a decision tree allows you to combine categories that have similar values with respect to the level of some target value there is less information loss in collapsing categories together. This leads to improved prediction and classification results. As shown in the figure, it is possible to intuitively appreciate that these collapsed categories can be used as branches in a tree. So, knowing the branch—for example, branch 3 (labeled BIN 3), we are better able to guess or predict the level of the target. In the case of branch 2 we can see that the target level lies in the mid-range, whereas in the last branch—here collapsed categories 1, 5, 6, 7, 9, 10—the target is relatively low.

Why Are Decision Trees So Useful?

Decision trees are a form of multiple variable (or multiple effect) analyses. All forms of multiple variable analyses allow us to predict, explain, describe, or classify an outcome (or target). An example of a multiple variable analysis is a probability of sale or the likelihood to respond to a marketing campaign as a result of the combined effects of multiple input variables, factors, or dimensions. This multiple variable analysis capability of decision trees enables you to go beyond simple one-cause, one-effect relationships and to discover and describe things in the context of multiple influences. Multiple variable analysis is particularly important in current problem-solving because almost all critical outcomes that determine success are based on multiple factors. Further, it is becoming increasingly clear that while it is easy to set up one-cause, one-effect relationships in the form of tables or graphs, this approach can lead to costly and misleading outcomes.

According to research in cognitive psychology (Miller 1956; Kahneman, Slovic, and Tversky 1982) the ability to conceptually grasp and manipulate multiple chunks of knowledge is limited by the physical and cognitive processing limitations of the short-term memory portion of the brain. This places a premium on the utilization of dimensional manipulation and presentation techniques that are capable of preserving and reflecting high-dimensionality relationships in a readily comprehensible form so that the relationships can be more easily consumed and applied by humans.

There are many multiple variable techniques available. The appeal of decision trees lies in their relative power, ease of use, robustness with a variety of data and levels of measurement, and ease of interpretability. Decision trees are developed and presented incrementally; thus, the combined set of multiple influences (which are necessary to fully explain the relationship of interest) is a collection of one-cause, one-effect relationships presented in the recursive form of a decision tree. This means that decision trees deal with human short-term memory limitations quite effectively and are easier to understand than more complex, multiple variable techniques. Decision trees turn raw data into an increased knowledge and awareness of business, engineering, and scientific issues, and they enable you to deploy that knowledge in a simple, but powerful set of human-readable rules.

Decision trees attempt to find a strong relationship between input values and target values in a group of observations that form a data set. When a set of input values is identified as having a strong relationship to a target value, then all of these values are grouped in a bin that becomes a branch on the decision tree. These groupings are determined by the observed form of the relationship between the bin values and the target. For example, suppose that the target average value differs sharply in the three bins that are formed by the input. As shown in Figure 1.4, binning involves taking each input, determining how the values in the input are related to the target, and, based on the input-target relationship, depositing inputs with similar values into bins that are formed by the relationship.

To visualize this process using the data in Figure 1.4, you see that BIN 1 contains values 1, 5, 6, 7, 9, and 10; BIN 2 contains values 3, 4, and 8; and BIN 3 contains value 2. The sort-selection mechanism can combine values in bins whether or not they are adjacent to one another (e.g., 3, 4, and 8 are in BIN 2, whereas 7 is in BIN 1). When only adjacent values are allowed to combine to form the branches of a decision tree, then the underlying form of measurement is assumed to monotonically increase as the numeric code of the input increases. When non-adjacent values are allowed to combine, then the underlying form of measurement is non-monotonic. A wide variety of different forms of measurement, including linear, nonlinear, and cyclic, can be modeled using decision trees.

A strong input-target relationship is formed when knowledge of the value of an input improves the ability to predict the value of the target. A strong relationship helps you understand the characteristics of the target. It is normal for this type of relationship to be useful in predicting the values of targets. For example, in most animal populations, knowing the height or weight improves the ability to predict the gender. In the following display, there are 28 observations in the data set. There are 20 males and 8 females.

Gender	Weight	Height	Ht_Cent.	BMIndex	BodyType
Female	179	4'10	147	162	slim
Female	160	5' 4	163	161	slim
Male	191	5' 8	173	182	average
Male	132	5'1	155	143	slim
Female	167	5'1	180	174	average
Female	128	5'2	157	142	slim
Female	150	5'2	157	154	slim
Male	150	5'2	157	154	slim
Female	215	5'2	157	184	heavy
Female	89	5'3	160	119	slim
Female	167	5'3	160	163	slim
Male	180	5'4	163	171	average
Male	206	5'4	163	183	average
Male	239	5'5	165	199	heavy
Male	161	5'6	168	164	average
Male	188	5'6	168	178	average
Male	284	5'6	168	218	heavy
Female	117	5'7	170	141	slim
Male	163	5'7	170	167	average
Male	194	5'7	170	182	average
Male	201	5'7	170	185	heavy
Male	254	5'8	173	209	heavy
Male	201	5'9	175	188	heavy
Male	206	5'9	175	190	heavy
Male	216	5'9	175	195	heavy
Male	206	6'0	183	194	heavy
Male	220	6'1	185	202	heavy
Female	182	6'2	188	185	heavy

In this display, the overall average height is 5'6 and the overall average weight is 183. Among males, the average height is 5'7, while among females, the average height is 5'3 (males weigh 200 on average, versus 155 for females).

Knowing the gender puts us in a better position to predict the height and weight of the individuals, and knowing the relationship between gender and height and weight puts us in a better position to understand the characteristics of the target. Based on the relationship between height and weight and gender, you can infer that females are both smaller and lighter than males. As a result, you can see how this sort of knowledge that is based on gender can be used to determine the height and weight of unseen humans.

From the display, you can construct a branch with three leaves to illustrate how decision trees are formed by grouping input values based on their relationship to the target.

Figure 1.5: Illustration of Decision Tree Partitioning of Physical Measurements

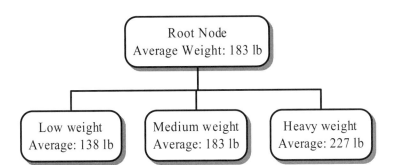

Level of Measurement

The example as shown here illustrates an important characteristic of decision trees: both quantitative and qualitative data can be accommodated in decision tree construction. Quantitative data, like height and weight, refers to quantities that can be manipulated with arithmetic operations such as addition, subtraction, and multiplication. Qualitative data, such as gender, cannot be used in arithmetic operations, but can be presented in tables or decision trees. In the previous example, the target field is weight and is presented as an average. Height, BMIndex, or BodyType could have been used as inputs to form the decision tree.

Some data, such as shoe size, behaves like both qualitative and quantitative data. For example, you might not be able to do meaningful arithmetic with shoe size, even though the sequence of numbers in shoe sizes is in an observable order. For example, with shoe size, size 10 is larger than size 9, but it is not twice as large as size 5.

Figure 1.6 displays a decision tree developed with a categorical target variable. This figure shows the general, tree-like characteristics of a decision tree and illustrates how decision trees display multiple relationships—one branch at a time. In subsequent figures, decision trees are shown with continuous or numeric fields as targets. This shows how decision trees are easily developed using targets and inputs that are both qualitative (categorical data) and quantitative (continuous, numeric data).

Figure 1.6: Illustration of a Decision Tree with a Categorical Target

The decision tree in Figure 1.6 displays the results of a mail-in customer survey conducted by HomeStuff, a national home goods retailer. In the survey, customers had the option to enter a cash drawing. Those who entered the drawing were classified as a HomeStuff *best* customer. Best customers are coded with **1** in the decision tree.

The top-level node of the decision tree shows that, of the 8399 respondents to the survey, 57% were classified as best customers, while 43% were classified as *other* (coded with **0**).

Figure 1.6 shows the general characteristics of a decision tree, such as partitioning the results of a 1–0 (categorical) target across various input fields in the customer survey data set. Under the top-level node, the field **GENDER** further characterizes the best – other (1–0) response. Females (coded with **F**) are more likely to be best customers than males (coded with **M**). Fifty-nine percent of females are best customers versus fifty-four percent of males. A wide variety of splitting techniques has been developed over time to gauge whether this difference is statistically significant and whether the results are accurate and reproducible. In Figure 1.6, the difference between males and females is statistically significant. Whether a difference of 5% is significant from a business point of view is a question that is best answered by the business analyst.

The splitting techniques that are used to split the 1–0 responses in the data set are used to identify alternative inputs (for example, income or purchase history) for gender. These techniques are based on numerical and statistical techniques that show an improvement over a simple, uninformed guess at the value of a target (in this example, best–other), as well as the reproducibility of this improvement with a new set of data.

Knowing the gender enables us to guess that females are 5% more likely to be a best customer than males. You could set up a separate, independent *hold out* or *validation* data set and (having determined that the gender effect is useful or interesting) you might see whether the strength and direction of the effect is reflected in the hold out or validation data set. The separate, independent data set will show the results if the decision tree is applied to a new data set, which indicates the generality of the results. Another way to assess the generality of the results is to look at data distributions that have been studied and developed by statisticians who know the properties of the data and who have developed guidelines based on the properties of the data and data distributions. The results could be compared to these data distributions and, based on the comparisons, you could determine the strength and reproducibility of the results. These approaches are discussed at greater length in Chapter 3, "The Mechanics of Decision Tree Construction."

Under the female node in the decision tree in Figure 1.6, female customers can be further categorized into best–other categories based on the total lifetime visits that they have made to HomeStuff stores: those who have made fewer than 3.5 visits are less likely to be best customers compared to those who have made more than 4.5 visits: 29% versus 100%. (In the survey, a shopping visit of less than 20 minutes was characterized as a half visit.)

On the right side of the figure, the decision tree is asymmetric; a new field—**Net sales**—has entered the analysis. This suggests that **Net sales** is a stronger or more relevant predictor of customer status than **Total lifetime visits**, which was used to analyze females. It was this kind of asymmetry that spurred the initial development of decision trees in the statistical community: these kinds of results demonstrate the importance of the combined (or interactive) effect of two indicators in displaying the drivers of an outcome. In the case of males, when **Net sales** exceed $281.50, then the likelihood of being a best customer increases from 45% to 77%.

As shown in the asymmetry of the decision tree, female behavior and male behavior have different nuances. To explain or predict female behavior, you have to look at the interaction of gender (in this case, female) with **Total lifetime visits**. For males, **Net sales** is an important characteristic to look at.

In Figure 1.6, of all the k-way or n-way branches that could have been formed in this decision tree, the 2-way branch is identified as best. This indicates that a 2-way branch produces the strongest effect. The strength of the effect is measured through a criterion that is based on strength of separation, statistical significance, or reproducibility, with respect to a validation process. These measures, as applied to the determination of branch formation and splitting criterion identification, are discussed further in Chapter 3.

Decision trees can accommodate categorical (gender), ordinal (number of visits), and continuous (net sales) types of fields as inputs or classifiers for the purpose of forming the decision tree. Input classifiers can be created by binning quantitative data types (ordinal and continuous) into categories that might be used in the creation of branches—or splits—in the decision tree. The bins that form total lifetime visits have been placed into three branches:

- < 3.5 ... less than 3.5
- [3.5 – 4.5) ... between 3.5 to strictly less than 4.5
- >= 4.5 ... greater than or equal to 4.5

Various nomenclatures are used to indicate which values fall in a given range. Meyers (2000) proposes an alternative, which is shown below:

- < 3.5 ... less than 3.5
- [3.5 – 4.5[... between 3.5 to strictly less than 4.5
- >= 4.5 ... greater than or equal to 4.5

The key difference from the convention used in the SAS decision tree is in the second range of values, where the designator "[" is used to indicate the interval that includes the lower number and includes up to any number that is strictly less than the upper number in the range.

A variety of techniques exist to cast bins into branches: 2-way (binary branches), n-way (where **n** equals the number of bins or categories), or k-way (where **k** represents an attempt to create an optimal number of branches and is some number greater than or equal to 2 and less than or equal to n).

Figure 1.7: Illustration of a Decision Tree—Continuous (Numeric) Target

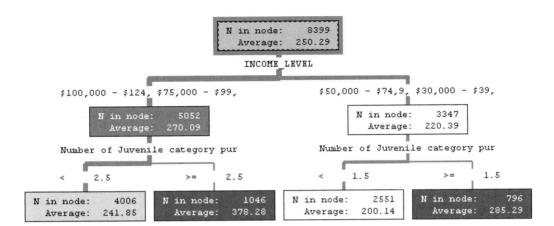

Figure 1.7 shows a decision tree that is created with a continuous response variable as the target. In this case, the target field is **Net sales**. This is the same field that was used as a classifier (for males) in the categorical response decision tree shown in Figure 1.6.

Overall, as shown in Figure 1.7, the average net sale amount is approximately $250. Figure 1.7 shows how this amount can be characterized by performing successive splits of net sales according to the income level of the survey responders and, within their income level, according to the field **Number of Juvenile category purchases**. In addition to characterizing net sales spending groups, this decision tree can be used as a predictive tool. For example, in Figure 1.7, high income, high juvenile category purchases typically outspend the average purchaser by an average of $378, versus the norm of $250. If someone were to ask what a relatively low income purchaser who buys a relatively low number of juvenile category items would spend, then the best guess would be about $200. This result is based on the decision rule, taken from the decision tree, as follows:

```
IF Number of Juvenile category purchases      <      1.5
AND INCOME_LEVEL       $50,000 - $74,9,
                       $40,000 - $49,9,
                       $30,000 - $39,9,
                       UNDER $30,000
                       THEN Average Net Sales = $200.14
```

Decision trees can contain both categorical and numeric (continuous) information in the nodes of the tree. Similarly, the characteristics that define the branches of the decision tree can be both categorical or numeric (in this latter case, the numeric values are collapsed into bins—sometimes called buckets or collapsed groupings of categories—to enable them to form the branches of the decision tree).

Figure 1.8 shows how the Fisher-Anderson iris data can yield three different types of branches when classifying the target SETOSA versus OTHER (Fisher 1936); in this case, 2-, 3-, and 5-leaf branches. There are 50 SETOSA records in the data set. With the binary partition, these records are classified perfectly by the rule **petal width <= 6 mm**. The 3-way and 5-way branch partitions are not as effective as the 2-way partition and are shown only for illustration. More examples are provided in Chapter 2, "Descriptive, Predictive, and Explanatory Analyses," including examples that show how 3-way and n-way partitions are better than 2-way partitions.

Figure 1.8: Illustration of Fisher-Anderson Iris Data and Decision Tree Options

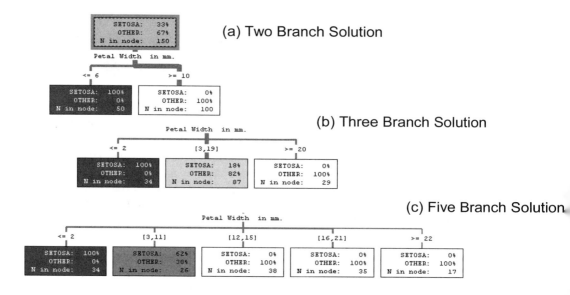

Descriptive, Predictive, and Explanatory Analyses

Introduction

In data analysis, it is common to work with data with descriptive, predictive, or explanatory outcomes in mind. A descriptive analysis could simply display a relationship in data or it could display the relationship as a graphic, such as a bar chart. The goal is to describe the data or a relationship among various data elements in the data set. This is common and normally the baseline point of departure in working with data to develop insight. For example, you could describe the weather by indicating the temperature, relative humidity, or atmospheric pressure.

Predictive use of data is a little different from descriptive use of data. In the predictive setting, it is normal to describe a relationship among data elements; furthermore, you can assert that this relationship will hold over time and be the same with new data, meaning that the relationship will be roughly reproduced in a novel situation. In the weather example, you can predict a weather effect based on the current rate of movement of a weather pattern, the differential pressure between competing weather systems, and air path measurements such as land mass, temperature, and humidity.

The explanatory use of data describes a relationship and attempts to show, by reference to the data, the effect and interpretation of the relationship. In the weather example, you could say that the effect of temperature on air mass humidity is rain or snow, depending on the degrees of temperature and the percent of humidity in the air (and other factors, such as atmospheric pressure and air particle concentration).

Typically, you must step up the rigor of the data work and task organization as you move from descriptive use to explanatory use. In a descriptive setting, the baseline goal is likely to be to present the facts in a clear and unambiguous fashion. In a predictive setting, the baseline goal is likely to be to produce a reliable and reproducible predicted outcome (which is usually confirmed by reference to validation or test data drawn from a novel, but related, set of circumstances as the host data used to train the predictive model). In a predictive setting, it is important to show the numerical relationship between predictive rules or equations and the target value. As a result, you can say that an increase in, for example, 10 units of a given predictor is likely to cause an increase in 2 units of the target or outcome of the prediction.

The explanatory use of data is more difficult to implement than either the descriptive or predictive use. Here, it is necessary to show how and to what degree a given relationship that is reflected in the data occurs. Usually, this demonstration is through reference to some explicit or implicit explanatory concept. For example, you can say that there is a direct relationship between air pressure and buoyancy of an air mass (or, for that matter, you can assert that there is a direct relationship between air pressure and the boiling temperature of water). Here, in the explanatory setting, you must show, through some kind of experiment, that the supposed relationship holds across various points of measurement, in different circumstances, and in different points in time. For example, if you describe the effect of air pressure on the boiling temperature of water, you might predict the boiling point at a given atmospheric pressure and then confirm the prediction through a measurement in an experimental setting. The most effective explanations demonstrate that the presumed relationship is primary, in that it is not an artifact of some preexisting relationship, nor is it mimicking the effects of an overarching or intervening relationship that is not expressed in the explanatory concept.

The Importance of Showing Context

Decision trees are constructed through successive recursive branches, where a branch is contained within the parent branch and is usually accompanied by peers that are formed at the same level of the decision tree. Because of this, a defining characteristic of a decision tree is that it clearly and graphically displays the interrelationships among the multiple factors that form the decision tree model, as viewed from branch to branch and between branches at any level of the decision tree. Decision trees display contextual effects—hot spots and soft spots in relationships that characterize data. These hot spots and soft spots reveal the frequently hidden and sometimes counterintuitive complexities in a relationship that unlock the decision-making potential of the data. For example, explore symmetry in branches that are peers at a given level of the decision tree: are sub-branches of a male gender split formed by the same inputs as sub-branches of a female gender split? In other words, are these relationships symmetrical? Is the direction of the relationship the same? Or, is there a reversal of the relationship—an interaction—that depends on the parent split?

You intuitively know the importance of multiple, contextual effects, but you often find it difficult to understand the context because of the inherent difficulty of capturing and describing the richly woven complexity of multiple, interrelated factors. It is tempting to resort to simpler models to describe relationships; however, as shown in the following example, this can produce misleading, maybe contrary, results.

Look back at the results of the decision tree in Figure 1.7. You might find it easy to conclude that the average purchase increases directly with the income level of the purchaser. This relationship is dramatically illustrated in the first branch of the decision tree. Average purchases increase from about $220 for those consumers whose incomes are $74,900 per year or less, to $270 for those consumers whose incomes are more than $74,900 annually. A better and more thorough understanding of this relationship comes from a closer examination of the various antecedents and intervening factors that could influence this relationship.

The term *antecedent* refers to factors or effects that are at the base of a chain of events or relationships, just as planting a seed can be an antecedent to measuring stem growth. An intervening factor comes between the ordering established by the other factors and outcome (for example, earth and water can serve as intermediate sprouting media to observe the effect of the planted seed on stem growth). Intervening factors can interact with antecedents or other intervening factors to produce an interactive effect. Interactive effects are an important dimension of discussions about decision trees and are explained more fully later. Decision trees show both main effects and interactive effects. For example, in Figure 1.7, the first level (branch) of the decision tree shows the main effect of income on purchases. The second level, under income, shows the interactive effect of income by number of purchases in the sales category of juvenile purchases.

Figure 2.1 displays a classic relationship observed between **X** and **Z**. **X** can represent any number of situations, events, states, or factors, usually captured on a data record. The same is true for **Z**. Antecedents, shown as **A** in Figure 2.2, include a variety of situations, events, states, or factors that precede **X** (conceptually or temporally), and **I** illustrates a variety of situations, events, states, or factors that could intervene between **X** and **Z**. Decision trees enable you to quickly explore your hypotheses about these relationships and to scan the data set for antecedents and intervening factors that might help you better understand the relationship between income level and amount purchased.

Figure 2.1: Illustration of Direction of Relationship

You might ask, "Does the relationship between income level and purchase amount depend on the gender of the customer?" (This question asks for an antecedent that might shed light on the relationship.) Or you might ask, "Does the relationship between income level and purchase amount depend on the number of average shopping visits in a year, or does it depend on the most recent purchase?" (This question asks for an intervening factor that could enhance your understanding of the relationship.) The results of looking at these two questions are illustrated in Figures 2.3 and 2.4.

Figure 2.2: Illustration of Antecedents and Intervening Factors

Antecedents

Figure 2.3 provides a concrete example of how an antecedent (in this case, gender) can affect the relationship between two other variables (income level and average purchase).

Figure 2.3: Illustration of the Effect of Other Factors

In Figure 2.3, the general form of the relationship confirms that females spend more, on average, than males, and spending increases with income level for both males and females. However, there is an anomaly in the spending of the high-income males; the $100,000+ annual income males actually outspend the same category of females—$286 versus $267. One interpretation of this effect is that the very best customers (in terms of purchase amount) are not high-income females, they are high-income males. This shows how decision trees can be used to test the effects of antecedents on the form of a relationship.

Intervening Factors

The decision tree in Figure 2.4 shows the effect of the intervening factor—latency—on the form of the relationship between income level and purchase amount. The term *latency* is borrowed from physics to describe the period of time that one component in a system is waiting for another component. In this case, latency refers to the period of time when the customer is outside the purchase cycle. Generally, the greater the latency (the time since last purchase), the lower the average purchase amount. This suggests that high-spending customers are also high-value customers.

An anomaly is revealed in the decision tree in the low-income group; among the 631 people included in the survey from low-income groups (incomes of $30,000 per year or less), the amount of purchase actually increases with latency (purchasers with latency in the >=90 day range out-spent those in the 60-day range). There are several interpretations of this phenomenon; for example, low-income customers may save up money to make planned-for purchases.

The important point to note is that intervening factors can mediate interrelationships between input variables, and decision trees provide a flexible method of examining how these effects can be accommodated in the interpretation and extraction of marketing knowledge.

Figure 2.4: Illustration of the Effect of Intervening Factors

---

A Classic Study and Illustration of the Need to Understand Context

Antecedents and intervening factors can have an important effect on the form of a relationship. Many documented cases show that this effect is substantial, and might involve a complete reversal in the direction of a relationship (e.g., from positive to negative), and can be both surprising and counterintuitive. A classic example is illustrated in the article "Simpson's Paradox and the Sure-Thing Principle," in the *Journal of the American Statistical Association* (Blyth 1972). To understand the scenario presented in this article, assume that you are a marketing manager for a software development/publishing company and that you are evaluating the effects of various promotional programs on long-term software retention. In Figure 2.5, you can see that the results to date have been particularly discouraging.[1]

---

[1] Figures presented in this example are, in general, the same as those in the original article. The variable names and scenario have been changed to reflect a marketing application instead of the epidemiological research application that was featured in the original article.

Figure 2.5: Illustration of Relationship Reversals—Baseline

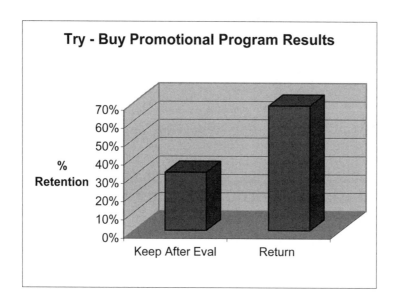

Figure 2.5 shows that a randomly selected group of respondents—11,000 were selected from advertisement responders and 11,000 were selected from information request responders—have a poor overall product retention (buy the product after an evaluation period) of only 32%. What is even more disturbing is that it was assumed that the information request responders would have a higher product retention because, presumably, these responders were better qualified than the responders from the general advertisement. The results on the source of the response are shown in Figure 2.6.

Figure 2.6: Illustration of the Effect of Third Variables

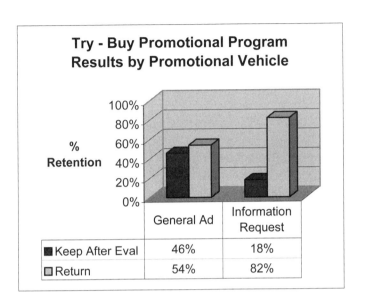

	General Ad	Information Request
■ Keep After Eval	46%	18%
□ Return	54%	82%

The marketing model assumed that, although it was more expensive to generate leads from articles and infomercials, these leads would be more likely to result in a better-qualified consumers than leads from general advertising, and that these leads would, in turn, have a higher retention rate.

The results presented in Figure 2.6 demonstrate that this marketing model was completely wrong...or was it? Are there other factors present and unaccounted for that would confirm the marketing model and perhaps indicate a successful program? In other words, are there other variables that capture contextual effects that need to be looked at to more accurately understand the relationship between retention and promotion?

The Effect of Context

So far, the results have been presented without considering all of the effects of possible predisposing or intervening factors in the presentation. One such factor—customer segment—has been excluded from the current analysis. Segment membership is recognized as an important component in the overall marketing program. Because of its importance, all customers are scored on a segmentation framework that was developed to chart the value of customers. As a result, customers are managed better and new customers can graduate to higher levels of customer value.

Segmentation makes a major distinction between the software's general users (generic) and higher-value power users. When the results of the promotional program are displayed, taking these two critical segments into account, a considerably different picture emerges, as shown in Figure 2.7.

Figure 2.7: Illustration of Relationships in Context

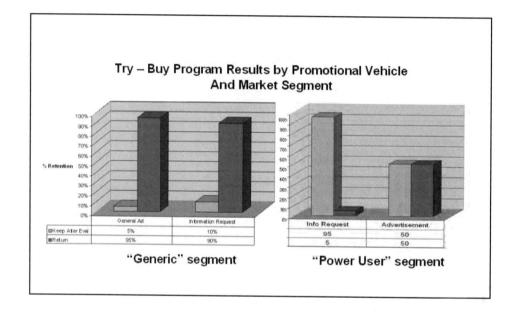

When results are presented with the important customer segments included, a different view is provided; in both customer segments, the information request promotional vehicle outperforms the general advertisement. In both customer segments, responders who were selected for the evaluation via the information request where about twice as likely to keep the software (10% versus 5% and 95% versus 50%).

How Do Misleading Results Appear?

How do the kinds of astonishing reversals of results, such as what it is in the "sure thing principle" (Blythe 1972), occur? How can decision trees be used to ensure the discovery and presentation of valid results? The decision tree could show some of the drivers of these reversal results. In Figure 2.8 the information request vehicle appears to confirm the original assumption: advertisements are a better source of renewed business.

Figure 2.8: Illustration of Advertisement vs. Information Request Promotion

If you look at the full decision tree in Figure 2.9, however, a different picture emerges. In the favored customer segment power users, the effect of information requests as a source of renewed business is very strong. Clearly, a decision tree application that is capable of sifting through the various interactions (combinations of antecedents and intervening factors that can influence the interpretation of relationships) would be useful.

Figure 2.9: Illustration of Full Decision Tree

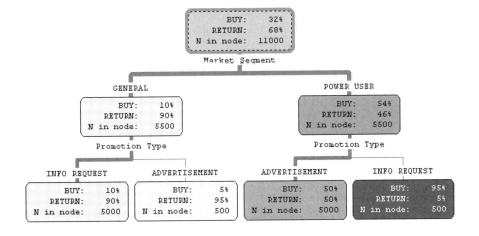

Automatic Interaction Detection

It is precisely this motivation that drove the results presented in a series of articles authored by the primary developers of decision tree software in North America—Morgan and Sonquist. They were economists working with economic indicators and predicting economic events at the Institute for Social Research at the University of Michigan in the late 1960s and early 1970s when they began to write a software program called AID (Automatic Interaction Detection). AID became the first decision tree program in North America.

Along with many other researchers at the time, they noted the same results that have been shown in previous examples—the form of a specific relationship is very much dependent on the context of the relationship and on the influence of other relevant factors in constructing and interpreting the relationship. They documented these observations in a seminal article in the *Journal of the American Statistical Association* (Morgan and Sonquist 1963). In this article, they suggested the use of decision trees to search through the many factors that can influence a relationship to ensure that the final results that are presented are accurate. The suggested approach evolved from a method of tabular analysis—a precursor to current-day multidimensional (OLAP) cubes—that was popular at the time. Although they were working within a regression framework, it is noteworthy that regression techniques, at that time, were in their infancy due to the limitations of computers. Even though Morgan and Sonquist were working with numeric data and regression models, they suggested an approach that was built on a style of contingency table analysis that had been developed by social scientists working on social theory and survey research analysis. This places this early development in the same context as current business analysts who may use regression techniques, but are more comfortable with developing and presenting results that are based on table views drawn from multidimensional cubes (for example, business intelligence and business analytics).

This style of analysis is a systematic attempt, in the examination of a relationship, to identify a preceding relationship (sometimes called a controlling or specifying relationship) that could change the nature or form of the relationship. This analysis approach was developed by P.F. Lazarsfeld and M. Rosenberg and was originally discussed in *The Language of Social Research* (1955).[2] Because of the limitations of computers at the time, it was common to conduct a tabular analysis of data. Data was

---

[2] Michael Weisberg, John Krosnick, and Bruce Bowen provide a more recent description of this method in *An Introduction to Survey Research and Data Analysis* (1989); however, the basic methodology remains unchanged to this day.

stored in 80-column punch cards, and the distribution of a field of data (column) in the card could be found by passing the data records (the card file) through a mechanical (rather than electronic) card sorter. This card sorter split up the records in a column into 10 bins, numbered 0 through 9. By counting the number of cards in each of the bins for a column, it was possible to derive the distribution of values for a field of information in the data set.

By applying this technique, it was also possible to successively partition the target of the analysis—say, income or dollars spent—according to the other fields in the analysis—for example, age of the study participants, gender, place of residence, and so on. The card sorter approach enabled the researchers to explore various subcategorizations of the target by looking at the results of various age–gender groupings and various age–gender–residence groupings, and so on. This approach produced the characteristic decision tree display that is now so familiar. Until the arrival of digital computers, this approach served as more computationally accessible compared to regression.

This approach was eventually adopted and embedded in the code that resulted in the development of the AID software program. As decision trees evolved, the goals of the approach expanded to handle both continuous and categorical table cell entries and multi-way branches. Statistical tests and validation approaches were later developed to assure the integrity of the decision tree.

In Morgan and Sonquist's approach, the type of intervening effect shown in the previous marketing example is due to an interaction between customer segment and the effect of the promotional program versus retention. The overall effect is negative, as you move from information requests to advertisements, with respect to keep versus return. Yet, the interaction displays subregions of the relationship that are dominated by the predisposing factor of customer segment. Within customer segment, the relationship is positive. In a term that was introduced by Lazarsfeld and Rosenberg, this is an example of a "controlling" relationship.

The concept of an interaction effect—or controlling relationship—is common in many modeling situations. As originally pointed out by Morgan and Sonquist, an interaction can obscure a strong relationship. In their article, they produced an example (Figure 2.10) where there is a relationship between savings and income—but only for the self-employed. There is an interaction between employment status and rate of savings. In Figure 2.10, the effect of employment status "specifies" the relationship between savings and income; it shows a more specific relationship among the various income categories.

Figure 2.10: Illustration of an Interaction Effect

Morgan and Sonquist proposed the use of this approach as an improvement over standard regression models. Thus, the automatic discovery of this kind of interactive relationship could be used to either grow a decision tree as an alternative to regression, or as a means to introduce interaction terms in the regression equations. The interaction term is used to segment the regression equation into two slopes; one slope captures the relationship between savings and income for the self-employed, and the other slope captures the relationship between savings and income for others.

Morgan and Sonquist noted that the decision tree approach provided an explanation of about two-thirds of the variability in the savings-income relationship, while the regression approach, even with interaction terms in the equations, accounted for only 36 percent of the variability. So, although decision tree results can be used to improve regression equations, these improvements may not perform at the same level as the original decision tree. This observation, and the resulting inquiry—and exposition of the relative merits of regression versus decision trees—prompted a lively discussion that continues to this day.

Morgan and Sonquist discovered and published an extremely important consideration regarding the complementarity and substitutability of regression and decision tree approaches: it is normal for decision trees to perform well with strong categorical, nonlinear effects. Even when these effects are used to enhance the regression equation, the regression results can still be inferior to the decision tree results. However, decision trees are inefficient at packaging the predictive effects of generally linear relationships and, in this situation, regression tends to perform better (and yield more economical models).[3]

Morgan and Sonquist discussed using the AID decision tree approach in dealing with another common problem with regression equations—multicollinearity. In multicollinearity, the relationships between the predictive terms in an equation obscure their effect on the target. This problem is shown in Figure 2.11. An appropriate remedy for multicollinearity is to respecify the regression equation (in this example, you would introduce a high–low savings term in the regression model to force separate slope estimates).

Figure 2.11: Illustration of Multicollinearity

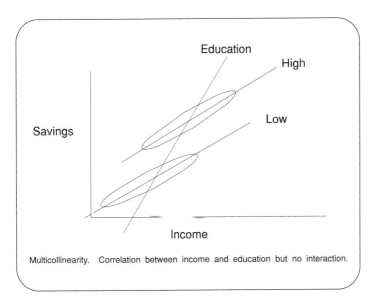

Multicollinearity. Correlation between income and education but no interaction.

Figure 2.12 shows how a regression model could be masked by a combination of both interactive and multicollinear effects. In this situation, decision trees would be immune to the model-defeating characteristics of these effects, and would be a useful tool in

---

[3] When a decision tree fits a linear relationship, it tends to fit the single line—represented by a slope coefficient in regression—as a series of decision tree branches. This tends to produce a line-fitting, staircase effect, which is neither economical nor as effective in prediction as regression is. Recent developments in multi-tree techniques, discussed elsewhere in this book, offset this disadvantage somewhat.

identifying terms for the regression equation to help the models perform better (and yield more interpretable results).

The power and utility of decision tree methods, and the original AID software program, is that both decision trees and AID addressed the problem of hidden relationships. This type of analysis technique proved to be very popular. The publication of Morgan and Sonquist's results, coupled with the availability of decision tree software (both in the United States and Europe), led to the development of decision trees as a stand-alone analysis technique. For many analysts, including statistical analysts, it became simpler and just as effective to use decision trees alone, which avoided the requirement of respecifying the regression equation. This decision tree popularity coincided with the growing power of computers and the ability of statistical analysts to move out of a tabular analysis framework and into a regression framework, or into a regression-augmented-with-AID framework.

Figure 2.12: Illustration of an Interaction with Multicollinearity

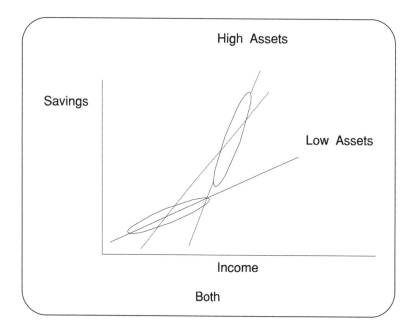

It should be noted that interpretability is sometimes overlooked as a desirable model feature in its own right, particularly as quantitative methods continue their migration into more general areas of business use. A decision tree display is often superior to the purely numerical display of the regression model because general users can recognize the qualitative and visual characteristics of a decision tree. By the same token, a general user can more easily recognize a regression-line display of a regression equation.

Figure 2.13: Illustration of Numerical, Regression, and Decision Tree Displays

Regression formulation:

$Y = 2X$

Decision tree rule form:

IF x_ < 70.5 THEN DO;
    Predicted y = 146;
    END;

Regression slope display:

Decision tree slope display:

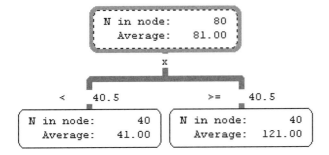

The Role of Validation and Statistics in Growing Decision Trees

Although it had several benefits and utilities, the AID decision tree approach developed by Morgan and Sonquist turned out to have major problems. The first problem was caused by the strength of the numerical-searching algorithm. Essentially, because the algorithm looks through so many potential groupings of values, it is more likely to find groupings that are actually anomalies in the data. Further, the successive partitioning of the data set into bins that form the nodes of the branches of the decision tree quickly exhausts the number of observations that are included in lower levels of the decision tree. As a result, the successively lower levels of the decision tree are based on an increasing number of assumptions about the splits that are used to form the branches. Also, due to the recursive nature of the decision tree algorithm, fewer data records and associated data points are used to identify the specific leaves or nodes that are formed by the branch splits or partitions.

Both problems—fitting anomalous relationships and fitting relationships with limited data—meant that it was not always possible to believe the efficacy of the branches that were identified by AID. This was pointed out as early as 1972 by Einhorn in an article that demonstrated that AID could form branches that reflected idiosyncrasies in the data, rather than reflecting effects in the population that the data represented. He pointed out that branches were formed based on a statistic that tried to minimize the variance within nodes and maximize the difference between nodes. The advantage of AID—looking through data and identifying any branch or split that could be used as an interaction—meant that many splits were formed and examined. This led to a "data-dredging" effect, where inputs formed branches with numerical values (branch partition values) that showed overstated results. These results were no more than artifacts of chance. The overstated results can be produced by the intensive computation to identify combinations of values that can be used to form branches of a decision tree. When many combinations are examined numerically, then it is usual to identify combinations that favor a particular view of the data that reflects the idiosyncrasies of the data, not the characteristics of the universe that the data was drawn from. This is the result even if the sample data is an accurate reflection of the universe that the sample data was drawn from.

An additional problem with AID was its tendency to find branches in inputs with large numbers of values, to the exclusion of branches in inputs with smaller numbers of values. This, too, was an artifact of chance and computation. For example, when looking for a binary split in a range of 100 values, AID would form a split for 1 versus 2+, 1-2 versus 3+, and so on. This process increases the chance that there will be at least one split along this range of 100 values that shows differences in a given target. In contrast, when exploring the relationship between gender, there is only one split possible—male versus female. If this branch does not produce a strong effect, then the algorithm will examine another input. There is less opportunity for chance to produce an effect (as there was with 100 values) and, consequently, there is less opportunity for fields with relatively few values to enter into the model when compared to fields with relatively more values.

Overall, three different kinds of problems were noted with AID:

- "Untrue" relationships (e.g., showing structure in random data)
- Biased selection of inputs or predictors
- AID did not know when to stop growing branches, and it formed splits at lower extremities of the decision tree where few data records were actually available

Because of its growing popularity and the utility of AID as an analysis tool, remedies to the problems were proposed. Remedies include using statistical tests to test the efficacy of a branch that is grown. For example, if a branch shows a difference between males and females with respect to an outcome, is this difference significant from a statistical point of view? Another remedy involves using validating data to test any branch that is formed for reproducibility. Hold out or validation data is typically formed by drawing a random sample from a data set before the data set is introduced into an analysis. The hold-out data is used to test any relationships that are formed with the original data (minus the hold-out data). Because the original data is used to form the relationship, it is sometimes called the "learning" or "training" data (because the algorithm "learns" the relationship).

One of the first remedies for addressing the problems with AID was proposed by Kass (1975). Kass suggested the use of statistical tests and Bonferroni adjustments. Bonferroni adjustments are named after the statistician who suggested that the level of statistical confidence of a statistical test be adjusted to account for the number of tests or trials that were used in producing the test. This provided a means to place inputs with 100 values or 2 values on the same footing. And it overcame the AID tendency toward the biased selection of predictors. These statistical tests also tested the reliability of branches formed in the AID decision tree, including the branches at lower levels of the decision tree.

Kass's approach was called CHAID. This stood for "chi-square AID". In conjunction with Hawkins (another statistician), Kass developed another approach, called XAID, which also used statistical tests, but worked with continuous targets (Hawkins and Kass 1982).

Remedies based on a validation approach were soon proposed by Breiman, Friedman, Olshen, and Stone (1984). Whereas the Kass approach used classical statistical theory to address the shortcomings of AID, the Breiman et al. approach relied on validation techniques to improve upon AID. Breiman et al. also introduced a number of new features. Their approach was called Classification and Regression Trees (CRT) and was published in a book of the same name.

The Application of Statistical Knowledge to Growing Decision Trees

Solutions based on Kass and Hawkins's methods began to appear in the late 1970s. The CHAID method works with a categorical response or target. The XAID method works with a continuous (or numeric) response or target. The general approach of their methods—referred to as CHAID analysis—allows for the development of decision trees with both categorical and numeric targets. The inputs to the analysis are used to form the attributes of the decision tree. The inputs, like the target, may be categorical or numeric. Although branches are formed as categories, Kass provided a method of dealing with numeric data that is at ordinal or interval levels of measurement. (It is usually possible to compress ordinal or interval data into a more restricted range of categorical values.)

Significance Tests

Statistical tests that are used in the CHAID analysis approach:

1. CHAID methods use a test of similarity to determine whether individual values of an input should be combined. With the age values, for example, if two age values have the same response value (from a statistical point of view, they are indistinguishable), then they are combined.
2. After similar values for an input have been combined according to the previous rule, tests of significance are used to select whether inputs are significant descriptors of target values and, if so, what are their strengths relative to other inputs.

The approach developed by Kass addresses all the problems in the AID approach:

1. A statistical test is used to ensure that only relationships that are significantly different from random effects are identified.
2. Statistical adjustments address the biased selection of variables as candidates for the branch partitions.
3. Tree growth is terminated when the branch that is produced fails the test of significance.

Kass introduced another innovation in the development of the form of the decision tree by describing how to form multi-way splits in the branches of the decision tree (as opposed to the simple binary or 2-way splits that form the AID decision tree). This multi-way splitting emerged as a result of Kass developing what he described as a merging-and-splitting heuristic in the construction of the branches of the decision tree.

The Role of Statistics in CHAID

CHAID relies on a traditional statistical test of significance to form the group boundaries that determine the values of the inputs that form the branches of the decision tree. Traditionally, the test of significance is constructed around the null hypothesis. When comparing the distributions of two or more groups in a data set, the statistician gathers numeric evidence to characterize the two or more groups and then poses the question, "Are there differences in magnitude among the groups so great that the null hypothesis of no differences can be rejected as not tenable?"

In practice, as greater magnitudes of differences are observed among groups, the statistician has more confidence in the structure and form of the relationship.

Confidence				
Extremely Good	Good	Pretty Good	Not So Good	Extremely Weak
.001	.01	.05	.10	.15

This test of significance determines which values are combined. The values are used as the various inputs that are considered as splitting criteria in the construction of the decision tree. To elaborate, a test of significance determines whether two values are the same with respect to their relationship to the target. If their values are the same, then they are combined. If their values are different, then they are separate branches on the decision tree. The significance test is illustrated in Figure 2.14. The degree of separation between two groups can be used as a test of the difference between two groups. The larger the separation, the stronger the relationship and, consequently, the greater the statistical confidence in the relationship. Because any two nodes on the branch of a decision tree can be seen as two groups, the internode separation can be tested with a test of significance. Multi-node tests can be used just as multigroup tests are used.

Figure 2.14: Illustration of Tests of Significance

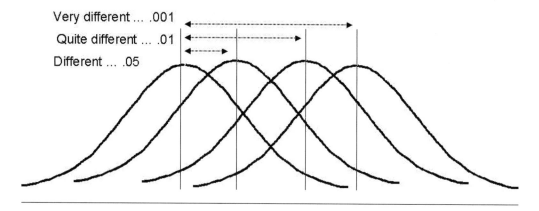

The second way that CHAID methods use statistics is to judge which relationships are strong enough to use in building the model. Once the values of a given input to the CHAID decision tree are combined through the merge-and-split method, then the resulting table can be set aside for subsequent evaluation. The process of combining field values for each input in the decision tree continues using the merge-and-split heuristic until, finally, all inputs have had their values combined.

Figure 2.15: Significance as a Function of Distribution Separations

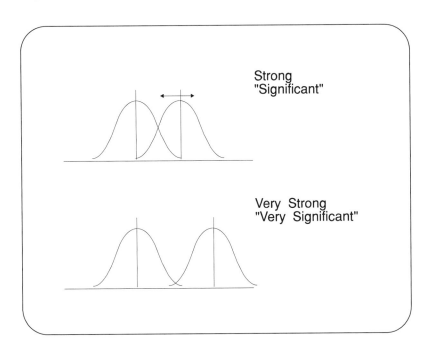

After the values of the inputs have been combined, you can look at each of the inputs and determine the overall statistical relationship between a given input, its associated branches, and the target to be predicted.

Kass proposed the use of statistical adjustments—referred to as Bonferroni adjustments—to eliminate the side effects of data-dredging. The level of statistical significance used to assess the identification of branches on the tree is adjusted. This adjustment factors in the number of tests that were conducted in identifying the relationship.

After Bonferroni adjustments have been applied, alternative partitions can be presented to the decision tree display, and the most appropriate input can be selected as the splitting criterion. In the absence of any other criterion, the input that is selected is the input with the highest Bonferroni-adjusted level of significance. Although this could be the best way to grow a decision tree from a predictive point of view, it might not be the best way to show the nature and sequence of relationships that characterize a given target. It is preferable for the analyst to grow the decision tree so that it supports the conceptual model that is being used to describe the target. So, when examining a list of alternative branches at a given level of the tree—all branches being significant—the analyst might choose the branch that best fits the conceptual model. This type of choice (from the SAS

Enteprise Miner interface) is shown in Display 2.1. In a banking application, a number of variables—such as IRA Balance, Age and so on—are potential inputs. Although the variable IRA Balance has the highest splitting criterion value (9.65622), there are many other variables that could be selected to grow the decision tree. Any of the variables could be used as a splitting criterion because all of them are significant from a statistical point of view. Selecting branches in a particular sequence has analogies in regression modeling, whereby the entry sequence of terms in a regression equation is determined by the analyst.

Display 2.1: SAS Enterprise Miner

Variable	-Log(p)	Bra
IRA Balance	9.656272E+0027	
Age	3.066892E-0037	
Investment	3.805094E+0017	
Checking Balance	1.225400E+0017	
Saving Balance	1.220559E+0017	
Checking Account	1.176964E+0017	
Safety Deposit Box	1.054413E+0017	
Money Market Balance	1.050095E+0017	
Money Market	1.035751E+0017	
Amount Deposited	0.200574E+0007	

Split Node 1 — Buttons: Apply, Edit Rule..., List All Variables, OK, Cancel

The measure of significance –**Log(p)** is a transformation of the normal method of displaying significance. This transformation is shown in the Glossary section of this book.

Validation to Determine Tree Size and Quality

While Kass was improving the operation of AID through tests of significance, parallel research and development was going on to validate data in the construction of decision trees. The results of this research and development were published by Breiman, Friedman, Olshen, and Stone (1984). The data validation approach developed by Breiman et al. was called Classification and Regression Trees (CRT).

CRT closely follows the original AID goal, but with improvement through the application of validation and cross-validation. In CRT, it is easy to determine where there is overfitting; as the decision tree is being developed, construct an algorithm to verify the reproducibility of the decision tree structure using hold-out or validation data. After a decision tree or a branch of a decision tree is grown, then reproduce the growth in the hold-out or validation data. If the validation results deviate from the training results, then the decision tree is not stable. Typically, the top level of the decision tree is readily reproduced; however, at lower levels of the decision tree, training results and validation results tend to deviate. And, at some level, the deviation is too severe to retain the form of the decision tree.

Breiman et al. found that it was not necessary to have hold-out or validation data to implement this grow-and-compare method. A cross-validation method can be used by resampling the training data that is used to grow the decision tree. This resampled data can also be used as a reference point—relative to the original or training data—to check and verify the accuracy and reproducibility of the tree as it is being grown.

CRT can include complexity (parsimony) to tune the size of the decision tree. With CRT, lower branches are penalized in the validation, which makes it harder to grow bigger trees that pass all the validation tests. In addition, it is possible to use prior probabilities to tune the size and shape of the decision tree. Here, the validation test is adjusted to reflect a distribution of the validation statistics that are calculated, so that the validation test is calculated on the basis of this distribution (rather than on the raw distribution, as reflected in the hold-out validation data).

What Is Validation?

Validation is a method of verifying the integrity (reproducibility) of a statistical model. Validation works by setting aside test data (typically 30%, selected randomly) that is from the original (training) data set used to develop the statistical model. This test data is subsequently used to test the performance of the model that is developed with the original (training) data. This form of validation is an alternative to resubstitution. Resubstitution uses data twice—once to grow the model and then again to test it. Simple methods of resubstitution overestimate the model's integrity.

Figure 2.16: Illustration of Validating Training and Test Data

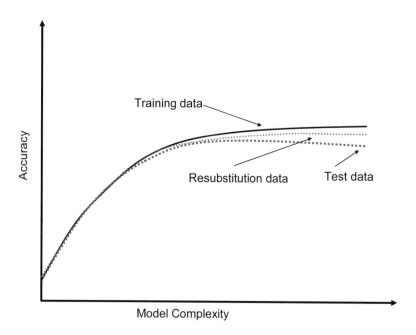

Regardless of the method used to validate the decision tree, you can assess the stability of the decision tree by comparing branch distributions of the target in the training and test data; if the test decision tree produces results that match the training decision tree, then there is confidence that the branches are reproducible and accurate.

In practice, training and test decision trees are built branch by branch. Comparisons between training and test decision trees are made with each successive branch that is built. Comparisons are made on the basis of deviations in the target values in the respective decision trees. If the target value is categorical, then the modal (most common) category predictions in the training decision tree are compared to the test tree. For interval targets, training mean values, as well as the variability between training and test samples can be compared for similarity. Comparisons are made on the basis of error rates.

At some point when growing branches, the error rates between training and test samples begin to diverge. As error rates climb the decision tree, the stability and reproducibility of the respective training and test trees at the lower branches deteriorate. When deterioration begins, it is time to stop growing the tree and select a subtree consisting of the higher branches that are more stable.

Figure 2.17: Illustration of the Grow-and-Prune Strategy

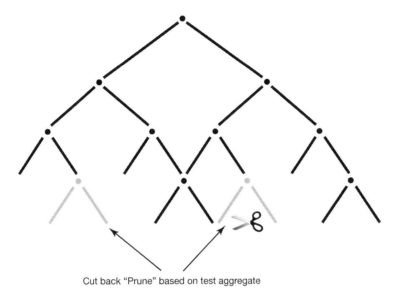

Cut back "Prune" based on test aggregate

The development of CRT laid the groundwork for these and many other validation approaches and provided tractable methods to grow reliable and accurate decision trees (what Breiman et al. called "honest" decision trees at the time). CRT solved the problems with the AID approach and proved as powerful a technique as the CHAID and XAID approaches developed by Kass.

The full methodology for growing and pruning branches in CRT include the following:

- For a continuous response field, both least squares and least absolute deviation measures can be used. Deviations between training and test measures can assess when the error rate has reached a point to justify pruning the subtree below the error-calculation point.

- For a categorical-dependent response field, it is possible to use either the Gini diversity measure or Twoing criteria.

- Ordered Twoing is a criterion for spitting ordinal target fields.

- Calculating misclassification costs of smaller decision trees is possible.

- Selecting the decision tree with the lowest or near-lowest cost is an option.

- Costs can be adjusted.
- Picking the smallest decision tree within one standard error of the lowest cost decision tree is an option.

In addition to a validated decision tree structure, CRT provided other extensions to AID:

- works with both continuous and categorical response variables
- handles missing values by imputation
- employs surrogate splits
- grows a larger-than-optimal decision tree and then prunes it to a final decision tree using a variety of pruning rules
- considers misclassification costs in the desirability of a split
- uses cost-complexity rules in the desirability of a split
- splits on linear and multiple linear combinations
- does subsampling with large data sets

Like AID, CRT employs a binary splitting methodology, which produces binary decision trees. CRT does not use the statistical hypothesis testing approach proposed by Kass, and CRT relies on the empirical properties of a validation or resampled data set to guard against overfit. Breiman et al. did not embrace the kind of merge-and-split heuristic developed by Kass to grow multi-way splits, so multi-way splits are not included in the CRT approach.

Pruning

The role of validation and pruning can be described using a decision tree run against a data set of banking transactions. The data set contains credit score as a target variable, and a number of inputs, including customer demographics, banking attributes (such as accounts used), and behavioral data such as transaction timing, counts, and monetary value. Figure 2.18 illustrates how a decision tree can grow with or without validation on the same data set (here, banking customers). As shown in the figure, a different approach to validation can produce dramatically different results.

Figure 2.18: Illustration of a Pruning Scenario

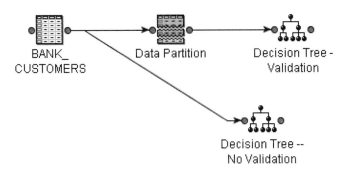

With a continuous target (such as credit score), a typical measure of decision tree model accuracy is to use an average squared error comparison between the training data set and the validation. The results are displayed in an iteration chart that shows the relationship between the average squared error computed as the decision tree creates leaf after leaf.

Display 2.2: Illustration of an Iteration Chart

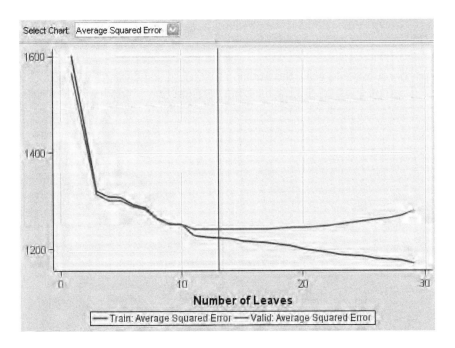

The training and validation data set decision trees yield a similar average squared error through the construction of 10 leaves, but they begin to diverge in the construction of leaves 11, 12, and so on. This results in the decision tree shown in Figure 2.19.

Figure 2.19: Illustration of the Effect of Pruning Decision Tree Growth

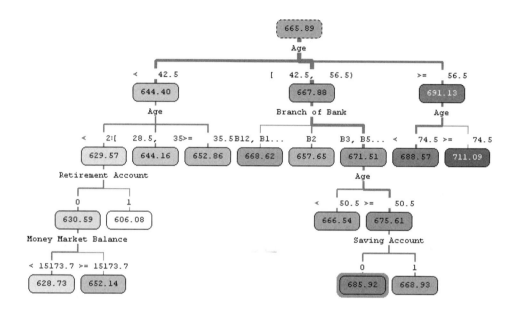

By contrast, if you were to grow the decision tree using standard branch-to-branch lookahead based on a test of significance, the decision tree would have more branches.

Figure 2.20: Tree Growth Using Significance Tests to Stop

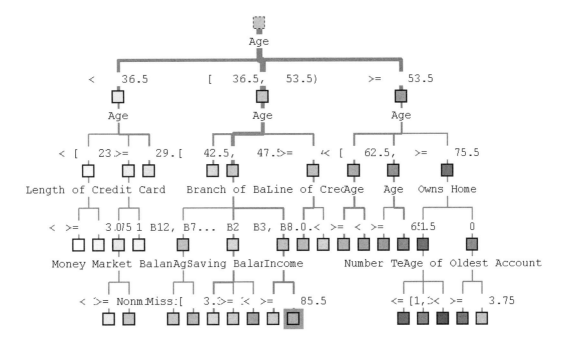

This decision tree has a total of 24 leaves, which is twice as many as what was produced using pruning as shown in Figure 2.19.

Decision trees have evolved significantly; however, early forms of decision trees laid the groundwork for many adaptations. The significant characteristics of these early decision trees are summarized in the following table.

Table 2.1: AID, CHAID, XAID, and CRT Compared

Technical Feature	AID	CHAID	XAID	CRT
Target variable - continuous	☐		☐	☐
Target variable - ordinal				☐
Target variable - categorical		☐		☐
Degree of branch partitioning	2	multi	multi	2
Splitting criterion adjusted for number of categories in predictor		☐	☐	
Splitting criterion adjusted for variable type (e.g., ordered, unordered)		☐	☐	
Criteria for splitting the node—for all possible 2-way splits, choose the one which explains the most variation	☐			☐
Criteria for splitting the node - for all possible multi-way splits, choose the one which explains the most variation		☐	☐	
To determine final decision tree stop: when too few observations	☐	☐	☐	☐
To determine final decision tree stop: when no more splits are significant		☐	☐	
Build a large decision tree and prune based on validation tests formed from test sample or resampling approach				☐
Split on linear combination of predictors				☐
Prior probabilities and cost function can be specified				☐

The entry "Split on linear combination of predictors" formed the basis of a number of enhancements in later years, such as the QUEST algorithm (Quick, Unbiased, Efficient, Statistical Tree). These enhancements are described by Loh and Vanichsetakul (1988). Although they are statistically powerful, these enhanced splits have never been adopted on a large scale. Splits that are made on a linear combination defeat one of the primary advantages of decision trees: ease of use and ease of interpretation and comprehension.

One of the early inspirations for decision trees—the Concept Learning System (CLS)—was proposed by Hunt, Marin, and Stone (1966). It inspired a parallel development of decision trees in the areas of machine learning and artificial intelligence. The connection between statistical approaches and approaches based on pattern recognition (including machine learning) has continued through the development of decision trees. In addition, this connection has been a robust source of innovation as decision trees have developed into a mature method of data mining.

Machine Learning, Rule Induction, and Statistical Decision Trees

Machine learning is a general way of describing computer-mediated methods of learning or developing knowledge. Machine learning began as an academic discipline. It is often associated with using computers to simulate or reproduce intelligent behavior. Example application areas include robotics, speech recognition, and language understanding and translation. Machine learning has also been used to build intelligent chess-playing programs (Shapiro 1987). Machine learning and business analytics share common goals: In order to behave with intelligence, it is necessary to acquire intelligence; further, it is necessary to acquire intelligence, and even refine it, over time as circumstances change. In these circumstances, there is a strong incentive to acquire intelligence from databases, which serve as records of positive and negative outcomes. An advantage of acquiring intelligence from databases is that the acquisition process can unfold in an automatic fashion. So, if data is accumulated less automatically, and if intelligence is extracted automatically, then it is possible to build and refine knowledge in ways that are not possible manually.

The broad goals of machine learning can be roughly compared to human learning goals: through the study of and experimentation with a particular area or subject, you can learn how the area or subject operates, how to react to it, and, possibly, how to exploit it to achieve whatever purpose you have in mind.

Knowledge can be captured and expressed in many ways and forms; for example, both collections of books and collections of data contain knowledge. Because data sets are usually more structured than books, they are a desirable source of knowledge for machine learning applications.

All decision trees are collections of rules. Although decision trees appear to be visual representations, if you look underneath, you will see that decision trees are rule expressions. Thus, every branch on the decision tree has a semantic description and because of this, decision trees are natural forms of machine learning. The development of decision trees to form rules is called *rule induction* in machine learning literature. *Induction* is the process of developing general laws on the basis of an examination of particular cases.

The areas of rule induction, machine learning, and statistical decision trees are closely linked. A good discussion of these areas and some useful references are provided by Michie (1991) and McKenzie et al. (1993). Many forms of machine learning work with data in an approach that is analogous to statistical approaches, and attempt to achieve results that are comparable to statistical results. Statistical approaches are used in the aspects of science that depend upon observations to confirm or deny objective indicators of the theories and hypotheses that explain events and phenomena in academic disciplines. Physical scientists often use empirical data to confirm their theories and hypotheses; for example, the continued effect of humidity on oxidation rates in various metal composites. Sciences of human behavior use empirical data to confirm theories; for example, increases in purchases in response to a lowered rate of interest or promotional discount. The role of statistics in these examples is often to assess the importance and reliability of the rules or relations that are discovered through the examination of the data. In this respect, the goals of statistics and machine learning are so aligned that, in many cases, they are indistinguishable (at times, they are similar disciplines with separate names). This is particularly true in the field of data mining, which explores the use of generally available data sources to extract knowledge, often in the form of rules, to illuminate a practical or academic concern.

Rule Induction

In the early years of the academic study of intelligence, it was common to think of knowledge and thinking processes as consisting of rules and the processing of rules. Humans, for example, could be considered rule processors who make decisions based on rules that they carry in their heads. So, if the weather is cool, you put on a warm coat. Early forms of machine learning were modeled after this conceptualization of human behavior. One of the earliest forms of machine learning was based on a form of rule induction called the Concept Learning System (CLS) and was developed by Hunt, Marin, and Stone (1966). Most forms of decision trees can trace their roots back to CLS.

Forms of rule induction inspired by the CLS algorithm (and the underlying concept learning model of Hunt, Marin, and Stone) most closely resemble statistical decision trees. Here, a concept is learned by discovering rules that can classify an object. An object is classified by discovering how variations in a criterion attribute can be predicted or explained in terms of the other attributes that have been collected or measured for the object.

In most applications of rule induction, the goal is to examine a set of cases to inductively derive predictive rules that allow you to characterize a situation with accuracy and reliability. For example, if you observe that in winter, at high altitudes, the temperature is lower, then you might propose the following predictive rule:

```
IF      season is winter
AND     altitude is high
THEN    temperature is low
```

Almost all computer systems that rely on machine learning contain at least some rules, and the majority of computer systems rely on rules to accomplish most of their main functions. A rule has the following form:

```
IF      <condition>
THEN    <action>
```

A condition can be a state that is determined by the results of an equality (for example, is age equal to 30 years?) or an inequality (for example, is hair color not blonde?) relationship.

Rules can be collected from experts or extracted from an appropriate data set. For example, in a medical expert system, a medical practitioner might propose a rule such as:

```
IF      temperature-elevated
THEN    prescribe-remedy
```

In this example, the rule reflects medical knowledge (and, in this case, conventional wisdom) that an elevated temperature usually indicates that the subject is fighting off an infectious organism, such as a cold, or has a bacterial infection; therefore, the subject requires some kind of remedy.

A study discussed by Ho Tu Bao (2002) provides real-world data on meningitis that was collected at the Medical Research Institute, Tokyo Medical and Dental University from 1979 to 1993. The database contains data of patients who suffered from meningitis and who were admitted to the department of emergency and neurology in several hospitals. A pattern discovered from this database is expressed in the form of rules:

```
IF     Poly-nuclear cell count in CFS <= 220
       AND   Risk factor = n
       AND   Loss of consciousness = positive
       AND   When nausea starts > 15
THEN   Prediction = Virus
```

Rules can be extracted from data quickly and inexpensively. If the data is structured appropriately, then the rules are not subject to human bias and can be thought to reflect objective truth. Data can be designed to quickly respond to and reflect the environment. Thus, rules extracted in this fashion are always up to date. In summary, rules generated by software possess many advantages.

- Because rules are extracted from data, they are objective and not prone to subjective interpretation; they are as good as the data they are extracted from and the extraction method that is used.

- Rules can be extracted automatically. Hence, they are less expensive.

- Because rules are extracted automatically, they can be produced quickly.

- Although subjective experience and domain knowledge often cannot keep up with changes in the environment (for example, new external market constraints, new technology, and so forth), data can if it is collected properly.

Improved methods of mineral exploration is one of the many uses of rule induction in the discovery of knowledge in data. This is illustrated by the work of the Geological Survey of Canada (Reddy and Bonham-Carter 1991). Reddy and Bonham-Carter have used an inductive approach to predict mineral deposits. A database contains information on the presence of a given mineral deposit. Each record in this database also contains information about the surrounding geology, gravity, magnetic vertical gradient readings, proximity to volcanic sites, and so on. By inductively examining the conditions that are associated with the presence of a mineral deposit, it is possible to formulate a rule that predicts the location of a mineral deposit. For example:

RULE_1

      IF   geology = mafic intermediate volcanics
      OR   mafic intrusives magnetic vertical gradient = 1 to 6

THEN

         no deposit = 86.6%
         deposit = 13.4%

RULE_2

      IF   geology = mafic intermediate volcanics
      OR   mafic intrusives magnetic vertical gradient = 7

THEN

         no deposit = 60.3%
         deposit = 39.7%

Both of these rules predict a higher likelihood of mineral deposit than the average of about 5% in the entire database. Information on the surrounding geology and magnetic vertical gradient readings enables the development of these predictive rules. These rules were developed using a decision tree.

Michie and Sammut (1991) have shown that not only can decision tree rules be used to examine remotely sensed data or medical records, but that they can examine physical behavior to derive a set of rules for balancing a pole, controlling a satellite, or even flying a plane. An article in *AI Magazine* (Michie and Sammut 1991) described their work with a pole and cart problem, shown in Figure 2.21.

Figure 2.21: Illustration of the Motion Dynamics in the Pole and Cart Problem

The pole and cart problem involves balancing a pole on a cart on a horizontal track that travels along a left-right axis. A human operator runs the pole and cart and is connected to a device that records the adjustments made to keep the pole balanced vertically. The human intervention forms a training set of data that contains rules that describe the adjustments.

Michie and Sammut applied the same process to controlling a satellite. The relationships in the data were more complicated because, unlike the two-dimensional adjustments made to the pole and cart, a satellite has pitch, yaw, and roll directions. Nevertheless, the process is similar. Here is a sample set of rules used to control a satellite's movements:

```
if ωz < -0.002 then apply torque of 1.5
else if ωz > 0.002 then apply torque of -1.5
else if pitch < -2 then apply torque of 1.5
else if pitch > 2 then apply torque of -1.5
else if ωy < -0.002 then apply torque of 1.5
else if ωy > 0.002 then apply torque of -1.5
else if roll < -2 then apply torque of 1.5
else if roll > 2 then apply torque of -1.5
else if ωx < -0.002 then apply torque of 0.5
else if ωx > 0.002 then apply torque of -0.5
else if yaw < -2 then apply torque of 0.5
else if yaw > 2 then apply torque of -0.5
```

Michie and Sammut call these implementations "adaptive control systems." They point out that the conventional control theory requires a mathematical model to predict the behavior of a process so that appropriate control actions can be made. An example of this type of mathematical model is shown in Figure 2.22.

Figure 2.22: Illustration of the Mathematical Model to Describe the Pole and Cart Movement

$$\ddot{\theta}_t = \frac{g \sin \theta_t + \cos \theta_t \left[\dfrac{-F_t - m_p l \dot{\theta}_t^2 \sin \theta_t}{m_c + m_p} \right]}{l \left[\dfrac{4}{3} - \dfrac{m_p \cos^2 \theta_t}{m_c + m_p} \right]}$$

$$\ddot{x}_t = \frac{F_t + m_p l [\dot{\theta}^2 \sin \theta_t - \ddot{\theta}_t \cos \theta_t]}{m_c + m_p}$$

$$x_{t+1} = x_t + \tau \dot{x}_t$$

$$x_{t+1} = x_t + \tau \ddot{x}_t$$

$$\theta_{t+1} = \theta_t + \tau \dot{\theta}_t$$

$$\dot{\theta}_{t+1} = \dot{\theta}_t + \tau \ddot{\theta}_t$$

Many processes are too complicated to model accurately. Often, not enough information is available about the process's environment. When the process is too complicated or the environment is not well-understood, an adaptive controller might work. An adaptive controller learns how to use the control actions available to meet the process's objective. The process is treated as a black box and the adaptive controller interacts with it by responses that have been learned through rule induction.

Rule Induction and the Work of Ross Quinlan

Rule induction was the inspiration for one of the most popular forms of machine learning, which was developed by Ross Quinlan at the University of Sydney, Australia. Quinlan developed one of the earliest top-down approaches to the rule induction of decision trees approach called "ID3". "ID" stands for "Interactive Dichotomizer" and "3" stands for "version 3", which was the most widely known version. More information and some useful references are provided by Michie (1991). Briefly, ID3 computes a gain ratio to determine the structure of the decision tree. The gain ratio functions like the variance reduction statistic in AID, or like the chi-square statistic in CHAID. ID3 is based on the concept of entropy, developed by Claude Shannon to describe the amount of information that is contained in a signal. Although this concept was originally used to describe the capacity of various communications channels, it can be used in decision trees to describe the communications capacity of competing splits or inputs and the resulting branches on the decision tree.

The ID3 algorithm had many of the same shortcomings as the AID algorithm; for example, decision trees might be grown too large to be reliable; multi-valued inputs could be favored over inputs with fewer values. Unlike AID or CHAID, ID3 did not combine similar values on the branches; if an input had three values, it produced a branch with three nodes, while a five-valued input produced five nodes, and so on.

The development of ID3 provided a significant boost for decision tree methods in machine learning. ID3 ultimately led to the introduction of more traditional, statistically based decision tree methods in a machine learning setting. This led to the continued development of decision trees in a variety of areas and applications—a development that continues to this day.

Improvements to the ID3 algorithm culminated in the development of the C4.5 method of decision tree construction, as well as its successor—C5.0. The C4.5 algorithm resolves problems identified in the original AID and ID3 implementations, and deals with both qualitative and quantitative attributes, missing values, and overfitting. C4.5 expanded the types of inputs possible—the target is nominal and the inputs can be either nominal or interval.

Unlike the ID3 algorithm, which produced n-way splits, the C4.5 decision tree algorithm produces binary splits. For multiple values, each attribute is first assigned to a unique branch, and then, in steps, two branches are merged until only two branches exist. Missing values are excluded from the split search on that input and from the numerator of the gain ratio. Missing values are an additional branch in the decision tree. For interval inputs, C4.5 finds the best binary split. For nominal inputs, a branch is created for every value, and then, optionally, the branches are merged until splitting does not improve the decision tree.

Merging is performed stepwise. At each step, the pair of branches that most improves the splitting measure is merged. When creating a split, observations with a missing value in the splitting variable are discarded when computing the reduction in entropy. The entropy of a split is then computed as if the split makes an additional branch exclusively for the missing values.

The decision tree is grown to overfit the training data. In each node, an upper-confidence limit of the number misclassified is estimated, assuming a binomial distribution around the number misclassified. A subtree is sought that minimizes the number misclassifications in each node.

C4.5 can convert a decision tree into a *rule set*. A rule set is a collection of rules that describe the leaves of a decision tree. An optimizer runs through the rule set so that similar rules are combined and redundancies are eliminated. Because these rule sets contain fewer rules than the decision tree, they are more readily understandable than most rule representations. In some cases, rule sets can be more readily understandable than decision tree representations.

C4.5 can create fuzzy splits on interval inputs. The decision tree is constructed the same as with non-fuzzy splits. If an interval input has a value near the splitting value, then the observation is effectively replaced by two observations, each with weight related to the proximity of the internal input value to the splitting value. The posterior probabilities of the original observation equal the weighted sum of the posterior probabilities of the two new observations.

The most recent version of Quinlan's approach is C5.0. C5.0 is an improvement over C4.5 and provides boosting and cross-validation. Boosting resamples the data that is used to train the decision tree. Each time the data is used to grow a decision tree, the accuracy of the decision tree is computed. Over time, data is adjusted to address previously computed inaccuracies. C5.0 provides facilities to specify number misclassification costs.

The Use of Multiple Trees

The mid-1990s were a watershed era for decision trees. In addition to Quinlan's work and the work of Breiman, Friedman, Olshen, and Stone, significant developments came from computer science. Two researchers, in particular, developed a new approach that became influential. The work of Amit and Geman (1991) on digit recognition involved using multiple decision trees to create what they called a holographic view of the digits in the source database.

This led to the development of a new class of decision tree approaches based on resampling and reweighting the original data to create a family of predictors that perform together better than single predictor. Multi-tree—or boost approaches—are discussed further in Chapter 4.

Amit and Geman compared their approach to creating a holographic view of the problem so that a given decision tree split could be viewed from various perspectives. The family of random decision trees that were grown from the original data is used to create these various perspectives.

Amit and Geman's work served as an inspiration to Quinlan, and most significantly to Leo Breiman, who developed this approach into random forests. The work on random forests is most notable because it represents decades of interaction between the machine learning community and the statistical community. This interaction is not always productive, possibly because of a difference in emphasis. As Breiman noted in the Wald series of lectures (2002): machine learning people tend to be interested in *whether things work*, whereas statisticians tend to be interested in *why things work*.

A Review of the Major Features of Decision Trees

So far, this chapter has described how decision trees have readily definable features that characterize and distinguish them from other data discovery, display, and deployment techniques. Decision trees were originally developed as robust yet simple methods to deal with the many complexities of multiple relationships among fields of information in data sets. These complexities and contextual effects are often missed by other methods of analysis, which can lead to inappropriate decisions. This is why decision trees, which explicitly discover and display multiple relationships in context, are such important tools for the empirical discovery, display, and validation of knowledge. The simplicity of decision trees facilitates the examination of multiple relationships, which enables decision trees to go beyond simplistic one-cause-one-effect types of analysis.

Roots and Trees

Decision tree results are produced graphically in the form of a decision tree. The normal display is an inverted tree with the root node at the top. The root node contains a summary of the data set to be examined; typically, it consists of the values of the field that will be partitioned or examined as the decision tree grows. Because this field is the target of the analysis, it is often called the target; however, because its values can be dependent on the values of the fields that will be used to examine it, then it can also be called a dependent field or variable.

Branches

Important inputs are selected as the splitting criteria in forming the shape and sequence of branches on the decision tree. The decision tree criteria separate important from unimportant branches so only strong relationships between inputs and the target are retained.

Inputs are referred to as predictors or classifiers because their values can be used to predict target values or classify target values. Whether inputs are predictors or classifiers, they are still considered inputs. Inputs have utility as a general descriptive term for predictors, classifiers, independent variables and, as is sometimes used in machine-learning applications, attributes. Branches can be 2-way (binary) or multi-way (many) and are formed by partitioning or splitting the target values with respect to the corresponding values in the inputs. Inputs can be any level of measurement—qualitative or quantitative.

Similarity Measures

Many measures have been used to select inputs and combine inputs that form partitions or classifications of the target. Attributes of the branches are grouped in the two or more nodes that characterize the branches. So, when a branch is identified with its associated leaves or nodes, then the members of each leaf or node are as homogenous as possible (with respect to their relationship with the target). In addition, each leaf or node is maximally distinguished or differentiated from other nodes on the same branch of the decision tree. Internode (between node) differences are maximized, and intranode (within node) similarities are maximized.

Typical statistical measures of association include a measure of how one set of values is related to or associated with another set; a measure of information gain (i.e., how much information about a target do I gain knowing corresponding information about an input?); or a measure or purity (how homogenous or diversified are the members of a branch of the tree?). It is possible to review the partitions or classifications formed by various inputs and to either select an input based on the numerical properties of the partitioning mechanism, or to select an input based on business rules.

Recursive Growth

Decision trees are said to be grown recursively; that is, once the initial or root node is split into a branch, all subsequent nodes are also split using the same methodology. So, once you discover how to split one node on a decision tree, you can recursively apply the same methodology to all descendent branches and associated nodes on the decision tree. Once a classification that is formed by the branches of an input is selected, the decision tree can be grown incrementally by descending to the nodes formed by this branch. This branch is, in turn, partitioned like the original root node was. This process continues as the decision tree is grown until it either runs out of data in the descendent node, or the growth is stopped according to a stopping rule. This is called recursive partitioning growth.

Shaping the Decision Tree

Various stopping rules can suggest when recursive partitioning should be stopped. It is necessary to stop at some point because deep decision trees are more complicated to understand and less useful. In addition, the lower branches are formed by fewer cases in the target data set; therefore, the statistical results are based on less statistical power and are consequently less accurate and reproducible. The validity, accuracy, and reproducibility of the decision tree can be tested through validation. Indeed, both validation testing can be used to shape the form and depth of the tree (including which input to use for branching and how many branches to form for a given input).

Deploying Decision Trees

The results, interpretation, and application of decision trees can be described, semantically, as simple IF <condition> THEN <action> rules. This way of describing relationships is very general and close to natural language, so it is readily understandable in non-scientific (i.e., non-mathematical) situations. In fact, these rules are virtually indistinguishable from the programming rules in many programming languages. In most cases, the rules are deployed in a markup language, such as PMML (Predictive Modeling Markup Language).

A Brief Review of the SAS Enterprise Miner ARBORETUM Procedure

The SAS ARBORETUM procedure is the computational engine that lies behind the decision tree construction that is found in SAS Enterprise Miner. The ARBORETUM procedure works with nominal, ordinal, and interval data as both inputs and targets in a decision tree. The ARBORETUM procedure forms branches in a decision tree using a variety of criteria, including:

- variance reduction for interval targets
- F-test for interval targets
- Gini or entropy reduction (information gain) for categorical targets
- chi-squared for nominal targets

The ARBORETUM procedure produces both binary and multi-way branches in the decision tree. Missing values in the input fields that are used to form branches can be handled in a variety of ways:

- use missing values as a separate, but legitimate code in the split search
- assign missing values to the leaf that they most closely resemble
- distribute missing observations across all branches
- use surrogate, non-missing inputs to impute the distribution of missing values in the branch

The ARBORETUM procedure provides a variety of methods for trimming and shaping the size and form of the decision tree, including:

- cost-complexity pruning and reduced-error pruning (with validation data)
- prior probabilities can be used in training or assessment
- misclassification costs can be used to influence decisions and branch construction
- interactive training mode can be used to produce branches and prune branches

The ARBORETUM procedure provides methods to compute variable importance, which can be done with both training and validation data. The ARBORETUM procedure provides for the generation of SAS programming code. This code can contain indicator variables that refer to specific leaves on the decision tree. These indicator variables can then be used as inputs to capture effects in other modeling applications. In addition, the generation of PMML code is provided.

The Mechanics of Decision Tree Construction

The Basics of Decision Trees

The goal of this section is to provide a comprehensive and detailed overview of the process of growing a decision tree. Many of the most common decision tree options and approaches are covered. These options and approaches have their roots in the original AID algorithm, as well as successor algorithms, such as CHAID, ID3, and CRT. The decision tree component of SAS Enterprise Miner incorporates and extends these options and approaches. It includes the popular features of CHAID and CRT and incorporates the decision tree algorithm refinements of the machine learning community (including the methods developed by Quinlan in ID3 and its successors).

The SAS Enterprise Miner decision tree supports both interactive (manual) and automatic growth approaches. Adjustable defaults are provided in both interactive and automatic approaches to help identify the best decision tree models for the analyst's purpose.

The decision tree growing process can be broken down into a number of subprocesses, as shown in Figure 3.1.

Figure 3.1: Illustration of Subprocesses in Growing a Decision Tree

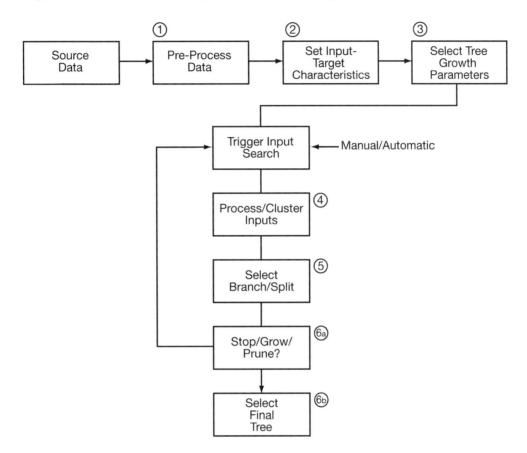

The six steps for growing decision trees are:

1. Preprocess the data for the decision tree growing engine.
2. Set the input and target modeling characteristics.
3. Select the decision tree growth parameters.
4. Cluster and process each branch-forming input field.
5. Select the candidate decision tree branches.
6. Complete the form and content of the final decision tree.
    a. Stop, grow, prune, or iterate the decision tree.
    b. Select the final decision tree.

These steps are performed in sequence, with the development of each layer of branches (or levels) of the decision tree. The decision tree growing process—steps 4 and 5—is an iterative process. This means that once the steps have been applied to the main set of data, which forms the root node of the decision tree, they can be reapplied recursively to any descendents of the root node.

Step 6—Complete the form and content of the final decision tree—is subject to both formal and informal shaping methods, which are used to terminate tree construction often before the mechanical components of the tree-growing algorithms stop functioning.

Step 1—Preprocess the Data for the Decision Tree Growing Engine

Data preparation is a study in its own right. There are books and courses on data preparation, for example, *Data Preparation for Data Mining* (Pyle 1999). It is frequently necessary to write code to preprocess the data. For example, the following SAS code transforms string abbreviations into numeric state codes:

```
IF substr(upcase(left(state)),1,2) in ("ME","NH","VT","MA")
THEN region = 1
```

Here are some rules-of-thumb for decision tree modeling.

1. Understand the differences between categorical and continuous data. Categorical data such as zip codes might have a numeric form with many values that can look like continuous data, but that are actually categories. Consider clustering categories together outside of the decision tree. It might be possible to cluster categories together with respect to a target variable (this is discussed later).
2. Categorical targets with more than two values are extremely difficult to interpret. Rework multi-category targets into a 1-of-N code scheme. With 1-of-N coding, each distinct category becomes a binary yes-no/on-off outcome in a new input. There are as many binary inputs as categories in the original multi-category input.
3. Dates can be a continuous field, but might need to be changed to Julian format. It is useful to compute time intervals, such as length of time as a customer, before beginning analysis.
4. There can be other time and distance measures; these need to be calculated and verified before analysis.
5. Try to avoid information loss; higher levels of measurement contain more information than lower levels, so actual income is preferable to income ranges.
6. If you are working with variables that are expressed along a scale, for example, 1, 2, 3, and so on, then you might find it easier to express all scales in the same direction.

7. Multiple response items might need to be treated with care. For example, if you have a list of products that are purchased, then each product might need to be totaled separately, and a total number of products purchased might need to be calculated. In this s, multiple response items within each unit of observation might need to be summed to create an analysis data set.

8. Do not confuse missing information with a missing value because this is not always the same. For example, Quantity Purchased can be blank for a given day or a given product type if the customer did not purchase on that day or did not purchase that product.

9. It might be necessary to pivot records, particularly if you want to compute purchase quantities for given products. The product purchases tend to be one-line-per-purchase records with purchase details and a customer number. The purchase details need to be summarized through a pivoting operation, such as PROC TRANSFORM. Then, the aggregates are attached to the record (typically using customer number as a key).

Once the data is available, display the attributes using a summarization routine, such as what is provided in the StatExplore node in SAS Enterprise Miner. The StatExplore node produces a good diagnostic summary of the attributes, as illustrated in the following output using the shopping data set from Chapter 2.

Variable	Numcat	NMiss	Mode	Pct	Mode2	Mode2Pct
RECENCY	8	0	30	20.17	60	17.38
children_home	3	10822	64.43	Y	33.17	
freq	7	0	5	47.59	4	23.21
gender	3	1839	female	58.95	male	30.1
has_new_car	2	0	N	63.51	Y	36.49
inc	10	2622	$100,000-$124,999	22.97	$75,000-$99,999	19.91
maritalStatus	2	0	Married	63.31	Self	36.69
money	18	0	200-299	16.12	100-149	15.19
occupation	10	7459		44.41	1	22.74
state	46	0	NJ	11.33	CA	10.31

Class Variables 1

Variable	Mean	StdDev	Non Missing	Missing	Min	Median	Max
NetSalesLife	248	283	16797	0	-4991	168	8493
adultsInHH	2	1	16797	0	0	2	6
age	47	13	15693	1104	18	46	96
bathroomPurchases	5	8	16797	0	0	2	240
bedroom	3	4	16797	0	0	1	74
couponPurchase	2	5	16797	0	0	0	105
display	2	3	16797	0	0	0	78
hasBankCard	1	0	16797	0	0	1	1
hasStoreCard	1	0	16797	0	0	1	1
has_card	0	0	16797	0	0	0	1
has_credit_card	0	0	16797	0	0	0	1
has_upscale_store_card	1	0	16797	0	0	1	1
income	6	2	16797	0	0	7	9
juvenile	2	4	16797	0	0	0	129
kitchen	2	4	16797	0	0	1	96
length_of_residence	7	5	15356	1441	1	6	15
lifeTransactions	21	18	16797	0	3	16	379
lifeVisits	4	2	16797	0	3	4	50
mystery_field	1	0	16797	0	0	1	1
owns_RV	0	0	16797	0	0	0	1
owns_motorcycle	0	0	16797	0	0	0	1
owns_truck	0	0	16797	0	0	0	1
table	1	2	16797	0	0	0	37
topIndicator	1	0	16797	0	0	1	1
valueOfCar	24	19	7743	9054	1	20	205
windowDisplay	5	6	16797	0	0	3	85

Interval Variables 1

The Segment Profile node in SAS Enterprise Miner produces profile results, as illustrated in Figure 3.2.

Figure 3.2: Distribution of the Target Values

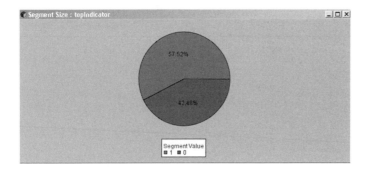

Or, assume that the data set has been defined and introduced into the data mining environment. The data set takes the form of a table with rows and columns. The rows represent individual records or observations. The columns contain measurements taken across each record or observation. So, each data line represents an object of analysis that has attributes with associated values.

Step 2—Set the Input and Target Modeling Characteristics

Decision tree inputs and targets can be encoded at any level of measurement, ranging from raw, nonmetric categories (such as high, medium, and low) to highly refined, precise, quantitative measurements (such as temperature in fractional degrees of Fahrenheit or Celsius). It is useful and necessary to preprocess the inputs and targets in order to do meaningful work with a decision tree.

One of the fields of the data set serves as the target of analysis. Other fields are defined as inputs that can be used to predict or describe this target of analysis. These inputs are columns of the table that are used as input variables to construct a set of decision rules. These decision rules describe or predict variations in the target.

Targets

Interval targets are the easiest to deal with. Almost all decision tree algorithms accept an interval target. In a data analysis task, you should always check the missing value indicator for the target field. Look for values such as –1, –99, and even 0 (which can indicate a missing measurement) and ensure that the target field is either removed from the analysis or handled appropriately.

Some fields such as SIC code or zip code can appear to be interval targets, when in fact they are categorical targets and, except under special circumstances, cannot be treated as interval targets. Variables can be treated as interval, only if the average value and deviations from the average value have meaning. In the case of SIC codes and zip codes, the average value of SIC codes or zip codes does not represent the average value of the codes that they are formed from. Therefore, averages and deviations from averages have no readily interpretable meaning for these codes.

With this type of categorical target, you create a 1-of-N derivation of the categorical codes. Thus, SIC code 8062 (hospitals) becomes 1 and all other target values become 0. This allows you to distinguish hospitals from all other target values in the analysis.

Similarly, zip code 10010 (for New York city) becomes 1 and all other target values become 0.

You should treat all categorical outcomes this way, even when a small number of categories could be modeled as an unmodified categorical or nominal target, such as a target with low, medium, and high category codes. (In this case, the target is also an ordered target.) The main reason for this recommendation is interpretability; it is very hard to understand the distribution of categories in the nodes of the branches of a decision tree when more than two categories are present.

The decision tree algorithm accommodates multi-valued categorical and ordinal targets so you can use them in the raw form. If you are interested in prediction, then the ability to read and interpret the nodes of a decision tree might be less pressing. Consequently, in predictive applications, the need to change multi-valued categorical and ordinal targets might not be great.

In the following example, height is the target variable that is set up as a function of various input variables (or inputs), which are used as distinguishing attributes to construct the decision rules that describe the functional relationship between target and inputs.

```
Height <--- I1, I2, ... , In   (For example, Gender, Age, ... ,
Hair color)
```

Height, which is the target, is called a target or dependent variable (meaning, because its value is a function of the input variables, it depends on the values of the inputs). Because the values of the inputs in this formulation can vary, they may be called independent variables.

Targets can be quantitative or continuously valued entities, such as height. Targets in nonmetric, nonquantitative, or categorical forms (such as short or tall) can also be used. As with targets, input fields can be any measurement, from nonnumeric categories (such as gender) to numeric quantities (such as weight and age). Numeric quantities can be used in both continuous and ordinal representations. For example, you can have age ranging from 0 to infinity (quantitative representation) or in one-year increments, such as 1 through life expectancy < 100 years.

Both targets and inputs can be unordered, such as State code. Decision trees are a useful and versatile method for handling many unordered inputs. Although decision trees have many flexible and powerful ways of handling multi-category targets, decision trees with more than two or three categories become difficult to work with and interpret.

Inputs

To prepare the data for decision tree analysis, SAS Enterprise Miner transforms the representation of inputs into discrete categories (e.g., age 15–25). All input values have to be able to form one of the branches of the decision tree and these branches are defined by discrete values of the inputs. Therefore, all input values need to be mapped to categories before analysis. For example, instead of using age as a continuously valued quantity (e.g., ranging from 5 to 85), age is transformed into an input with discrete categories. Categories are determined by the following:

- interval ranges (e.g., a natural range such as lower school, middle school, and high school in education)
- buckets, bins, or grouping rules (e.g., groups formed by interval ranges)
- quantiles (e.g., equal frequency groups formed by ranked quantities)

A discrete category is the age category of 15 to 25. This age value is substituted for all age values in the data set that are in the range of 15 to 25 (inclusive). This step is necessary because age, as an input, has to take on values that can form groups or classes of values on the branches of the decision tree. In most cases, this means that the values need to be set up as classes of values (i.e., the level of measurement must be categorical).

The SAS Enterprise Miner decision tree can take a parameter that determines the number of bins (called "n" in the following equation). This parameter indirectly specifies the minimum width between two successive candidate split points on an interval input. The width equals $(\max(x) - \min(x))/(n + 1)$, where $\max(x)$ and $\min(x)$ are the maximum and minimum of the input variable values in the within-node sample being searched. The width is computed separately for each input and node.

You could classify a field like age into 10 buckets or bins to turn it into a categorical field. It is also possible to define your own preset collapsed categories. For example, age can be classified into the following groupings:

Preteens	< 13
Teens	13–19
Young adults	20–29
Older adults	30–55
Seniors	> 55

In general, numeric fields can be classified in the following ways:

- in defined ranges (as previously shown)
- as buckets or bins, in which the number of records in each bucket or bin depends on the definition of the bin attributes and the mapping process that assigns individual records to each bin in the data set
- as deciles or other quantiles, in which there are an equal number of records in each decile group

If a quantile has been defined, then binning is based on the frequency of records that are in a quantile range. Quantiles are computed by taking the frequency of each value in the input. The quantile is formed by establishing a lower and upper quantile value that encompasses the number of records that form the quantile. So, if a decile is computed, then the first decile contains 10% of the input records according to the frequency of occurrence.

In addition to establishing all input values as categorical fields, you must establish whether the categories are ordered or unordered. Age is ordered or monotonic—there is a steady increase in the magnitude of age as you move from the lowest category (e.g., preteens) to the highest category (e.g., seniors).

However, if you use the values of State as input, then you would define this input as nominal or unordered. There is no innate underlying increase or decrease in the assumed magnitude of a State code as you move from IA to AL, or, if the State codes are assigned a number, as you move from 12 (representing the state of New York) to 25 (representing the state of Montana), there is no increase or decrease.

Step 3—Select the Decision Tree Growth Parameters

Although there are many decision tree algorithms, forming a decision tree is a simple process. Originally, decision trees were formed by sorting inputs into ordered groupings. The sort order was a function of the value of the input category, with respect to the value in the target. With a continuous target, input categories were sorted from low to high, and the corresponding average target value was recorded in each of the input categories. If the input categories were combined to form a node that represented multiple categorical values, then the input categories were combined either ordered or unordered.

This original decision tree process begins by transforming each ordinal and interval type of input into categories that can be manipulated and combined.

Once all inputs are transformed, the decision tree algorithm performs its most important task—picking the best input to form a split. A number of choices affect this task. The more important considerations are the following:

- How will input categories be combined to form branches or will they be combined at all?

- How will branches be sorted and combined? Will they be in line with their level of measurement—continuous, ordinal, and categorical?

- How many nodes on a branch will be allowed?

- How many alternative branches will be stored at each level of the decision tree?

- How will differences be determined (for example, predictive power between branches)?

- How will branches be evaluated, selected, and displayed?

- How will input data records be segmented into branches? What will happen when a given input data record has missing information in the input field that is being used to form a branch?

- Will a branch growth strategy be based on empirical tests of accuracy or will theoretical tests (for example, hypothesis tests) be used to grow branches?

- Will branches be pruned ahead of time or will branches be trimmed after an initial growth stage or once an overly large tree has been grown?

- When will the decision tree processor stop identifying potential branches?

- When will the decision tree stop identifying potential nodes?

A number of settings determine how to act on these considerations. For example, the total number of potential split-and-merge points in a range of bins for an input is an important setting. A split-and-merge point is a potential cutting point between two bins or categories of an input that can be merged to form a larger bin. Because the bins have different target attributes (which means they have different input-target behavior), categories are split apart. A typical default is to examine 5,000 potential split-and-merge points. If there are 5,000 or fewer points to examine, then SAS Enterprise Miner exhaustively examines all possible points. If more than 5,000 points exist, then a heuristic merge-and-shuffle approach is used. A merge-and-shuffle approach examines approximate groupings of categories so that the branches capture differences in the input-target behavior.

Various measures of computing the strength of a branch are used. Branches can be picked based on strength or based on validation and test statistics. The strength value is referred to as the "worth" of a branch. Typically, higher worth branches are picked over lower worth branches.

The decision tree mechanism in SAS Enterprise Miner treats missing values in different ways. The mechanism can: 1) include missing values, 2) put missing values into a separate category, 3) distribute observations with missing values in proportion to the size of the nodes on a branch, and, 4) use surrogate inputs in place of missing values. A surrogate input performs like an input, but has a lower worth. A surrogate input is highly correlated with the missing value, and forms the branch partition when there is a missing value for the input on the data record that is making the split. In this case, a non-missing surrogate input value on this data record can be used. You can set the maximum number of surrogates that can be used in growing the decision tree because when surrogates are used, the data has to be re-read (and this takes more time).

Nodes can be constrained to a minimum size, and any category in the target classification can be constrained to a certain size. For example, a constraint can be that no nodes with less than 50 observations will be identified, and no node with a categorical value with less than 5 observations will be identified.

Decision trees can be constrained to grow to a certain depth. For example, decision trees can be constrained to stop growing after 3 levels. Levels are calculated from the root node (in the example, the first set of branches forms the first level).

Inputs can be constrained to be used on only one level, so once they are used, they cannot be used again on a lower level.

Step 4—Cluster and Process Each Branch-Forming Input Field

Clusters of codes are formed when values in the input fields that form the branches of the decision tree are grouped together. The goal of this step is twofold:

1.   Put similar observations into the same cluster so that the characteristics of the observations in that cluster are as similar as possible. Create clusters on the same level of the split on the tree so that the differences between clusters are magnified. Create clusters of codes that make intuitive or theoretical sense (as when State codes are arranged into East, Central, West, North, and South).

2. Clustering forms nodes on the input that maximize the predictive relationship between the input and the target. This is the original and persistent goal of forming leaves on the input. However, this goal is sometimes at odds with the first goal because the most appealing or most understandable branch is not always the best predictor. In this case, the analyst has to choose between numerical strength and interpretability.

The result of the clustering step is the selection of an algorithm and the guidance rules that form the branches that, in turn, form the decision tree. One exception to this step is the rare case in which no input codes are grouped together (such as when the ID3 algorithm is running). The setting in SAS Enterprise Miner that controls this step is the maximum number of branches. For example, a setting of 2 to 50 will accommodate the construction of branches with 2 to 50 nodes or leaves.

When the maximum number of branches is set to 2, the decision tree is a binary tree. A number greater than 2 results in multi-way branches. Binary branches are easier to calculate. Input values are clustered on one of two sides when forming the decision tree branches—either on the left side or on the right side. The main question is whether the categories of the inputs are clustered in an ordered or unordered way. With ordered comparisons, adjacent categories in the range of categories in an input can be combined. With unordered comparisons, any category in an input can be combined with any other category. These different comparisons produce different results, as shown in Figure 3.3 and Figure 3.4.

In Figure 3.3, a decision tree shows the relationship with YOJ (Years On the Job) and its influence on the target variable in the analysis—bad debt. This decision tree is from the Home Equity Loan data that is provided in the sample Help files with SAS.

Figure 3.3: Illustration of Clusters Producing Two Nodes

All values lower than or equal to 5.6 are on the left side of the branch; all values greater than or equal to 6 are on the right side. In Figure 3.4, an unordered search for branches in the YOJ variable is shown.

Figure 3.4: Illustration of Binary Partitioning with Unordered Branch (Cluster) Components

When unordered clustering is used, out-of-sequence values can combine. In Figure 3.4, the value of 4, which would usually be in the sequence between 2.5 and 4.5 on the left side of the decision tree, has been grouped with the value of 7 on the right side of the decision tree. If you look at the distribution of YOJ versus bad debt, as shown in Figure 3.5, you can see this process at work.

Figure 3.5: Illustration of Bad Debt Distributed by YOJ - Ordered Search

The first five vertical bars have an elevated BAD count when compared to the bars that follow (in this example, BAD=code 1). In an ordered comparison, you would expect to see a split in the left and right branches, between the fifth and sixth bars. At this point, the cumulative number of bad counts is greater than the cumulative number of bad counts to the right (i.e., sixth bar and greater). This is exactly what is in the decision tree with the ordered split in Figure 3.5 (the split is at value 5.6). However, in an unordered search for left and right clusters, you would see that the fourth bar has a lower proportion of bad debts when compared to the bars in the sequence of low values less than 6. The unordered search algorithm has determined this and has grouped the value 4 on the right side of the decision tree.

All of these results are preliminary and unverified and are based on samples, not the data set. They are provided to illustrate the differences between ordered and unordered searches. After you begin to examine the distribution of values, you might find potential combinations of values that SAS Enterprise Miner has not detected. The comprehensive search of all possible values is covered in the discussion of search algorithms that follows.

Clusters of input values that form multi-way branches are more difficult to calculate than binary branches. However, multi-way branches have useful, visual, and conceptually appealing properties that make them more robust, economical, and flexible, especially in explanatory and expository decision tree applications. To explain further, suppose a decision tree breaks out sales into West, South West, Great Lakes, North East, and South East regions. All regions can be represented on one level of the decision tree with one decision rule. Binary trees would need to segment the data four times, with corresponding decision rules, to accomplish this. With multi-way branches, however, there are the issues of how many multi-way nodes to create, and where to establish the cutting points in the clusters that form the multi-way nodes.

Clustering Algorithms

A variety of clustering algorithms can form the branches that define the leaves in the decision tree. All algorithms try to create leaves that are as alike as possible (i.e., pure or homogeneous) and that are as different as possible when compared to other leaves on the same level of the decision tree. Observations in a leaf are similar, and differences between observations in leaf-to-leaf comparisons are as great as possible. Choosing an algorithm depends on the measurement of the input values that are grouped together.

- continuous-type measurements need quantity measures of clustering (to determine similar group members)
- categorical-type measurements need categorical measures of clustering (to determine similar group members)

The clustering algorithms most commonly used are the following:

- variance reduction (used in the original AID)
- entropy (adopted by Ross Quinlan)
- Gini (introduced by Breiman et al.)
- tests of significance (introduced by Kass)
  - o t-test and F-test for continuous measures
  - o chi-squared test (Fisher's exact test for small numbers) for categorical measures

When tests of significance are used, Bonferroni adjustments can be applied. Bonferroni adjustments compensate for measurement and test effects that force changes in the one-test/one-hypothesis approach. This approach forms the basis of traditional tests of significance and, consequently, the statistical tables that are published that reflect the underlying mathematics of these tests. This multi-test adjustment was originated by Kass (1976). It addressed shortcomings with the original AID algorithm and with the variance reduction test that was used to form the resulting decision tree. Specifically, these tests do the following:

- compensate for multiple tests of significance (affect the presentation order of potential branches)
- adjust the statistical strength of any input in the analysis to compensate for the number of inputs that are used to form potential branches (for example, asking "Is it a significant relationship?")
- adjust the stopping rule that is used to stop growing the tree (if a statistical test of significance is used as a stopping rule)

Variance Reduction

After the data is preprocessed (so that, for example, all continuous inputs are arranged as categorical inputs), the effect of each input is examined. The goal is to cluster the attributes of the inputs together, based on the strengths of their relationships with the values of the target. In the original AID decision tree approach, variance reduction was used to form binary groups or clusters for each input in the data set. Values were chosen so that variations from the average values of the two groups formed by the binary branch were minimal.

Gender	Height	Weight	BMI
male	68	203	31
female	59	94	19
female	64	113	19
male	64	160	27
female	67	125	20
female	64	120	21
female	64	120	21
female	67	134	21
female	63	125	22
male	65	135	22
female	65	135	22
male	67	144	23
female	67	145	23
female	57	105	23
male	68	150	23
female	68	150	23
male	66	143	23
female	62	128	23

(continued)

male	71	170	24
female	63	138	24
male	65	148	25
female	62	135	25
male	65	155	26
male	65	160	27
female	62	97	18
male	67	175	27
male	63	160	28
male	62	155	28
male	64	180	31

In the previous display, the mean and variance of BMI (Body Mass Index) are 23 and 11, respectively. BMI is calculated as weight divided by height, squared. Variance is the sum of the deviations of the individual measurements around the mean or average of the measure. If BMI is segmented into males and females, then the mean and variance are as follows:

	Number	Variance
Female	21	4
Male	26	9

Segmenting the BMI scores into females and males can reduce the variance in the resulting groups when compared to the overall variance. Gender is an important discriminator and is a likely candidate for splitting criterion in the decision tree.

Gini Impurity

The Gini index is a measure of variability/purity for categorical data. It was developed by the Italian statistician Corrado Gini in 1912. The Gini index can be used as a measure of node impurity, where p_1, p_2, ... , p_r are the relative frequencies of each class in a node. The Gini criterion was proposed by Breiman et al.

$$\textbf{Gini impurity} = 1 - \sum_{j}^{r} p_j^2$$

A pure node has a Gini index of 0—as the number of evenly distributed classes increases, the Gini index approaches 1. The splitting criterion is the one that most reduces the node impurity. In the following example, the impurity of the root node when considering body type is shown:

1 – (average purity measure) – (heavy purity measure) – (slim purity measure)

The Gini index is computed as follows:

$$1 - (\tfrac{8}{28})^2 - (\tfrac{11}{28})^2 - (\tfrac{9}{28})^2 \quad \text{or .82}$$

Gender	Weight	Height	Ht_Cent.	BodyType
Female	89	5'3	160	slim
Female	117	5'7	170	slim
Female	128	5'2	157	slim
Male	132	5'1	155	slim
Female	150	5'2	157	slim
Male	150	5'2	157	slim
Female	160	5' 4	163	slim
Female	179	4'10	147	slim
Female	167	5'3	160	slim
Male	161	5'6	168	average
Male	163	5'7	170	average
Male	180	5'4	163	average
Female	167	5'1	180	average
Male	188	5'6	168	average
Male	191	5'8	173	average
Male	194	5'7	170	average
Male	206	5'4	163	average
Female	215	5'2	157	heavy
Male	201	5'7	170	heavy
Female	182	6'2	188	heavy
Male	201	5'9	175	heavy
Male	206	5'9	175	heavy
Male	206	6'	183	heavy
Male	216	5'9	175	heavy
Male	239	5'5	165	heavy
Male	220	6'1	185	heavy
Male	254	5'8	173	heavy
Male	284	5'6	168	heavy

A split on gender produces two nodes with impurity measures of .48 and .89 (for females and males, respectively). This is a reduction in impurity of .41.

Entropy and Information Gain

Entropy was developed as a measure of the uncertainty of a transmitted message, in bits (Shannon 1948). Entropy is used with categorical outcomes—it measures variability (homogeneity) in splits and the leaves that are formed by the splits.

The entropy of a split is found by computing the entropy in each of the leaves, and by summing the entropy of all the leaves of a split. The variability of an outcome in a leaf is computed using the formula **-log$_2$(p$_i$)**. The summed entropy of all the leaves of a split is

$-\sum_{i=1}^{r} p_i \log_2(p_i)$, where p_i is the proportion of a particular class i in the collection of categories contained in the branch.

This measure is calculated as follows. The decision tree has 28 observations. The probability of body type is 8/28 (0.29), 11/28 (0.39), and 9/28 (0.32), for average, heavy, and slim, respectively. To compute the entropy, sum the three $\sum_{i=1}^{r} p_i \log_2(p_i)$ terms. The results are –0.51639, –0.52954, and –0.52632, with a summed entropy of 1.57. You can use other splits among the categories in the table, such as gender. For example, the entropy for males is 1.382 and for females is 1.156. The total entropy for gender is 1.30 and the information gain is .27 or 17%. You can verify these results with the following display:

Body Type	Frequency	Percent	Cumulative Percent
average	8	28.57	28.57
heavy	11	39.29	67.86
slim	9	32.14	100
	28		

For body type, the best guess for the 28 observations is **heavy**. The likely outcome to classify the body type is 11 right guesses versus 17 wrong guesses, which results in a classification hit rate of about 40%.

bodytype	Gender (Gender) Female	Male	Total
average	1	7	8
	3.57	25	28.57
	12.5	87.5	
	10	38.89	
heavy	2	9	11
	7.14	32.14	39.29
	18.18	81.82	
	20	50	
slim	7	2	9
	25	7.14	32.14
	77.78	22.22	
	70	11.11	
Total	10	18	28
	35.71	64.29	100

Knowing the distribution of gender increases the ability to guess correctly. For males, the best guess is **heavy**; for females, the best guess is slim. Using this guessing strategy means that you could get 9 guesses for males wrong, and 3 guesses for females wrong, which results in a classification hit rate of 57%. This yields an improvement of about 40%, equal to the information gain previously calculated.

Chi-Squared

The clustering process in the CHAID approach to forming a decision tree is based on applying a test of significance. In CHAID, input groupings are formed by combining values in the input if their relationships with the target are similar. Values are indistinguishable from a statistical point of view if the pair-wise differences between two values relative to the target are not statistically significant. Statistical significance can be determined by a simple t-test that tests the differences between the average values of the target for one input value versus another input value. If the test is not significant, then the two values are combined.

Ordered comparisons require pair-wise comparisons of adjacent values. If the test of significance fails, then the values are combined to form one category.

Unordered comparisons require pair-wise comparisons of all available values, regardless of order. If the test of significance between the two selected values fails, then the values are combined to form one value.

When selecting the test of significance, the test that is applied depends on how the values of the target are measured. Are they categorical (for example, yes–no) or are they numeric (for example, dollars spent)? For categorical targets, the usual test of significance is the chi-squared test (denoted X^2). For numeric targets, the usual test of significance is the t-test.

Figure 3.6: Illustration of a Test of Significance between Means

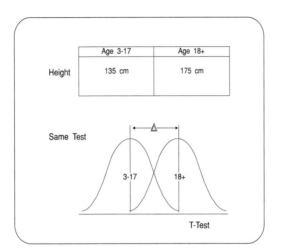

Tuning the Level of Significance

The level of significance affects whether the test succeeds or fails. Different branch targets are produced if different levels of significance are used to perform the test to establish the groupings. Statisticians have evolved rules for selecting the level of significance to use to perform a test. The .05 level of significance is an example. According to this test, the categories that are being compared are collapsed together if they cannot be shown to be significantly related to the value of the target at the 95% level of statistical confidence.[1]

Many other levels of significance can be used—for example, the .01 level (a more conservative test) or the .10 level (a more liberal test). In practice, as more conservative tests are applied to the construction of groups, greater differences between individual levels of encoding need to be observed for these codes to be considered for forming a separate leaf. The net effect is that the selection of the level of significance affects the bushiness of the decision tree and the homogeneity of clusters (in CHAID methods only). At higher levels of statistical significance, it can be hard to reject the null hypothesis of no differences between distributions (i.e., there is not enough separation between their

---

[1] The 95% level of statistical confidence asserts that the difference in the two distributions is so sufficiently large (or abnormal) that you would see this effect only about 5% of the time **by chance alone**. Because the likelihood of seeing it by chance is small (i.e., 5%), the statistical conclusion is to assert that the relationship is significant.

distributions); therefore, many codes are collapsed together. This results in a smaller number of leaves, illustrated in Figure 3.7.

Figure 3.7: Illustration of Branch Granularity as a Function of Cluster Similarity Measures

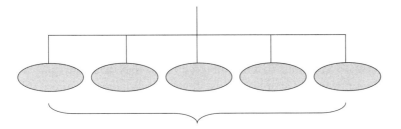

Fine grain (produced with higher levels of significant differences)

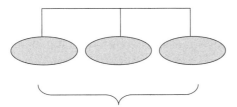

Coarser grain (produced with lower levels of significant differences)

Observation Selection

As the decision tree is grown, successive samples of data set values are used to form the branches of the decision tree. Tree-growing settings determine the number of observations (records) that are taken to form the sample. In the simplest case, all observations are taken to form the sample. However, it is not necessary to take all observations, for example, if the host data set is large. A sample containing less than all observations in the data set can yield identical or equivalent results to the full data set. When samples are taken, it is normal to take independent samples at each node of the decision tree. For nominal targets, it is normal to try to balance the sizes of the outcome categories. For example, suppose a node contains 100 observations of one value of a binary target, and 1,000 observations of another value. If the sample size is set to 200 or more, it makes sense to take all 100 observations of the first target, and to take a random sampling of the other target, until the sample of 200 observations is created. In calculating binary splits, the best binary partition of binary and interval targets is always found.

The creation of multi-branch decision trees is more complicated because of the numerous potential splits (compared to simple, binary splits), You should first consolidate the data before applying the method to evaluate all potential splits or, if a large number of potential splits seems likely, you should use a heuristic search for the best split. A consolidation phase searches for values of the input that would likely be assigned to the same group or cluster in the best split. Simple clustering can be used for consolidation (for example, group all input values that have the same or similar target value). The split-search algorithm treats observations in the same group as if they have the same input value. This results in a faster split search because fewer candidate values need evaluating.

The Kass Merge-and-Split Heuristic

In the development of the CHAID algorithm, Kass specified a merge-and-split heuristic to develop multi-branch trees. The merge-and-split heuristic tries to converge on a single, optimal clustering of like codes. This heuristic begins by merging codes within clusters and reassigning consolidated groups of observations to different branches. Then, the merge-and-split heuristic operates as a consolidation algorithm—the consolidated groups are broken up (by splitting out the members with the weakest relationships). These broken-up groups are remerged with consolidated groups that are similar.

The effect of the merge-and-split heuristic is to look at fewer potential combinations of values than would be required by a complete evaluation of all the potential combinations. The process stops when either a binary split is reached or there are no consolidated groups that can be split and merged at the similarity level specified by the algorithm.

SAS Enterprise Miner uses a variation of this heuristic called merge-and-shuffle. The merge-and-shuffle algorithm begins by assigning each consolidated group of observations to a different node. At each merge, the two nodes that degrade the worth of the split the least are merged. After two nodes are merged, the algorithm considers reassigning consolidated groups of observations to different nodes. Each consolidated group is considered and the process stops when no consolidated group can be reassigned.

When using the chi-squared test and F-test criteria, the p-value of the selected split on an input is subjected to more adjustments: if the adjusted p-value is greater than or equal to the worth value, the split is rejected.

Although the merge-and-split heuristic developed by Kass is designed to find a single solution, Biggs et al. (1991) realized that all the intermediate products that are formed in the merge-and-split process can be stored and, subsequently, evaluated for worth. Then, from all the candidate splits that are stored, the one split with the best worth can be chosen.

Dealing with Missing Data and Missing Inputs in Decision Trees

When forming groups from the values of the inputs, it is common for a data record to contain a missing value. This is almost always true in live data sets, regardless of the amount of data quality and data scrubbing. The net effect is that if the target or input value is missing, it is usually ignored.

In a multivariable technique like decision trees, missing values can lead to a considerable loss of data; once a data record is dropped at any stage of the decision tree growth process, all other data that is available in the data record is lost. For example, a missing value at the top level of the decision tree will cause the data record to be dropped, as well as any other input fields.

Clearly, you would want to recover as much of the data as possible in a data record. A number of methods for dealing with missing values in decision trees have been developed.

- treat a missing value as a legitimate value (i.e., explicitly include it in the analysis)

- use surrogates (i.e., another input) to populate descendent nodes where the input value for the preferred input is missing

- estimate the missing value based on non-missing inputs (i.e., treat the missing value category as a target value that can be estimated and, in a two-stage process, include the estimated value in the analysis—the simplest form of this method is to estimate the missing value as the average value for the input)

- distribute the missing value in the input to the descendent node based on a distribution rule (i.e., distribute the missing value to the most common descendent node)

- distribute missing values over all branches in proportion to the missing values by branch

During the search for a split, it is possible to use a missing value as another value when calculating the worth of a split. One advantage of using missing values during the search for splits is that the calculation of the worth of a split is computed with a larger number of observations for each potential split. Another advantage is that, even if there are missing values, this information can increase the predictive accuracy of a split. For splits on a categorical variable, this concept is the same as treating a missing value as a separate category. For continuous (numerical) target splits, this is the same as treating missing values as having the same (unknown) value.

This approach was developed in the original CHAID. A statistical test considers the missing value as another code that is grouped with the class that it most closely resembles (or, the missing values can be grouped into a separate class of their own). There are three variants to accommodate categorical (ordered and unordered) and continuous inputs (ordered, unordered, and floating variations).

An approach pioneered by CRT is to use surrogate splits when there is a missing value for the preferred branch on the decision tree. The input variable to form the split can be missing for an input data record. Other input variables are available (maybe not as strong, but still good) that can be used to determine whether that row of data (observation) goes to the right or the left of the node that is being split. This alternative input variable or surrogate is used to determine where the missing data record is assigned in the descendent node. Both surrogate and competing input variables are alternatives to the input variable that has been selected to form the splits that determine the descendent nodes. Surrogate splits are used only to distribute parent data records to descendent nodes when the selected input variable has missing values that prevent the distribution of records to nodes based on input values. In this case, the surrogate record values determine where to distribute data records in descendent nodes.

Imputation has long been used as a method to handle missing values. The distribution of the valid values for a field in the data set can be defined as a function of a set of inputs in the decision tree or regression form. This means that a predictive equation in the decision tree or regression form is available to produce a score for any target on any record as a function of other fields or inputs in the record. Thus, the values in any field can be considered a function of the values in all the fields in the same data row or record. The predictive equation in the decision tree or regression form can make predictions about unknown situations. A missing value is an unknown situation, so it can be predicted or imputed using this method.

The rules to distribute missing values to descendents in SAS Enterprise Miner are the following:

- distribute missing values across all available branches
- assign missing values to the most correlated branch
- assign missing values to the largest branch

In the distribution approach, data records are distributed to branches in proportion to the size of the branch. Thus, a branch with 50% of the observations, based on valid values, would receive 50% of the data records that contain missing values. (The data records are selected at random.) This method preserves all of the available information and reflects that information in proportion to the size of the branch that it is associated with. This concept is similar to substituting the average value for the decision tree analysis variables whereby the average value is weighted according to the probability of occurrence.

Surrogate Splits

When a split is applied for an observation with a missing value, it is possible to look for surrogate splits on another value before assigning the observation to the branch with the missing values. This surrogate-splitting rule is a backup for the main splitting rule. For example, the main splitting rule uses county. The surrogate-splitting rule uses region. If the county is unknown for a given observation, then region is used in its place.

If several surrogates exist, then when an observation for the main splitting rule is missing, each surrogate is considered in sequence until one can be applied to the observation. If no surrogate can be applied, the main splitting rule assigns the observation to the branch with the missing values.

The surrogates are considered in the order of their agreement with the main splitting rule. The agreement is measured as the proportion of training observations that it and the main splitting rule assign to the same branch. The surrogate rules saved in the decision tree run options to determine the number of surrogates that will be sought. A surrogate is discarded if it has a low agreement with the main splitting rule. A low agreement is less than or equal to 1, divided by the number of branches in the main split. As a result, a node might have fewer surrogates than the number specified in the surrogate rules saved in each node option.

Other characteristics of the calculation of the agreement can be noted. The agreement measure applies only to observations that are valid for the main splitting rule. Of these observations, any instances where the surrogate rule cannot be applied count as observations that do not get assigned to the same branch as the main splitting rule. Thus, an observation with a missing value in the observation used in the surrogate rule, but not in the observation used in the main splitting rule, counts against the surrogate.

Step 5—Select the Candidate Decision Tree Branches

Once the clustering is complete for all inputs that are being considered as branches at a level of the decision tree, then the inputs can be arranged in a list and ranked according to their predictive or classification power. The measure of power depends on the splitting criterion. In the previous illustration of the calculation of entropy, worth is calculated as the sum of the node computations across a branch. This calculation is used for entropy, Gini, and variance reduction. The test statistic is weighted by the proportion of observations contained in any node of the branch. Prior probabilities can be specified, and if these prior probabilities are incorporated in the split search, then the proportions are modified accordingly.

The chi-squared test and F-test criteria use the worth measure to assess the split. Worth is derived from the traditional p-value that is calculated for these test statistics, and is computed by taking the –log of the p-value. For the test criteria, the best split is the one with the smallest p-value (highest worth). The threshold value (p-value)—used to determine the significance of the test statistic and called the alpha level, which corresponds to the probability of a type I error—is set to .20 by default. The .20 level is liberal by most academic standards (where alpha levels of .05, .01, and even .001 are commonly used), but is considered appropriate in exploratory data mining work. Results need to be confirmed through validation or test trials.

The p-values may be adjusted to account for multiple testing. An approach that follows the original work of Kass is usually used. These adjustments to p-values can be reflected in the display if the adjustment option has been selected. If the Kass adjustment is applied before the split is selected, then the best split is the one with the smallest Kass-adjusted p-value. For nodes with many observations, the algorithm can use a sample for the split search, for computing the worth, and for observing the limit on the minimum size of a branch.

Adjustments can be applied after the split is selected. In this case, the unadjusted worth value is used to select the split. Split worth statistics, shown in the display, may use the Kass-adjusted p-values. Because the Kass adjustments reflect the level of measurement and the type of search, it is believed that the relative worth of inputs is more correctly reflected by adjusted worth measures, and the analyst is less likely to be deceived by the apparent value of a split.

The CHAID Approach

In the CHAID approach, it is common to apply a test of significance to the tables that are formed by each clustered input. The outcome of that test is then used as a measure of the quality of the branch that is formed by that input. The inputs are presented as partition candidates to form the branch of the decision tree at that level of the decision tree growth, in order of statistical confidence based on the test of significance. Statistical adjustments are applied to variables with many categories—ordered and unordered variables are compared on the basis of an adjusted metric so that the metric can be equitably applied to all inputs, regardless of the form of input.

Figure 3.8: Illustration of an F-Test on Multiple Means

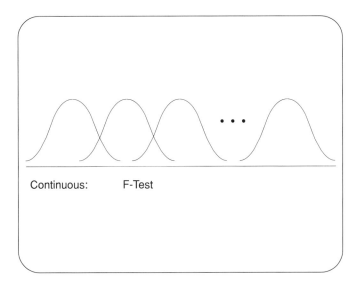

For numeric targets with interval-level measurements, the usual test of significance applied to the candidate branches of the decision tree is the F-test. The F-test provides a measure of between-group similarity versus within-group similarity. Similarity is assessed by measuring the variability of scores around the mean or average values in a descendent node, compared to the variability between the average values across the nodes of a branch.

The F-test calculation is a ratio of the between-node variability (sum of squares) versus the within-node variability. The degrees of freedom are *n* (the number of observations) and *B* (the number of branches). As shown in Figure 3.9, a ratio is calculated and assessed for significance to determine a p-value or test metric. The significance test uses measures to reflect statistical degrees of freedom, which provides a common way to look at numerical comparisons across different numbers of nodes on a branch and different numbers of observations.

Figure 3.9: Illustration of the Calculation of the F-Test

$$F = \left(\frac{SS_{between}}{SS_{within}}\right)\left(\frac{n-B}{B-1}\right) \sim F_{B-1,\,n-B}$$

The expression for computing the sum of squares between and the sum of squares within is the following:

Figure 3.10: Illustration of the Calculation of Sum of Squares Between

$$SS_{between} = \sum_{i=1}^{B} n_i \left(\bar{y}_{i.} - \bar{y}_{..}\right)^2$$

Figure 3.11: Illustration of the Calculation of Sum of Squares Within

$$SS_{within} = \sum_{i=1}^{B} SS_i = \sum_{i=1}^{B}\sum_{j=1}^{n_i}(y_{ij} - \bar{y}_i)^2$$

In the context of a decision tree, the F-test statistic can be viewed as a measure of deviation of the child leaves of a split, compared to the parent as a function of the pooled variability within the child leaves. The F-test statistic can be used to find branches that have nodes that are distinct from one another, and that have node members that are as homogeneous as possible.

For categorical targets, the usual test of significance applied to the candidate splits is the X^2 (chi-squared test). This test examines the cells of a table, looking for disproportionate numbers of observations in the cells. This happens when greater or fewer observations occur in the cell than would be expected if the observations were distributed randomly. The value of the test statistic increases as more observations collect in one or more cells in disproportionate numbers.[2] In Table 3.1, the relationship between gender and car

---

[2] The X^2 test was developed for row X column tables. It is appropriate for a decision tree because a partition on a decision tree is, in fact, a row X column table (where the values of the target form the rows and the values of the partitions form the columns). This similarity between decision trees and tables is reflected in the use of decision trees for multidimensional cube analysis. In fact, a decision tree can be viewed as a multidimensional cube.

ownership is shown. Approximately 36% of females (3,606) own a new car, while about 38% of males (1,939) own a new car.

Table 3.1 Relationship between Gender and Car Ownership

Gender and New Car Ownership			
Owns new car	**gender**		**Total**
	female	**male**	
No	6296	3117	9413
(percent)	63.58	61.65	
Yes	3606	1939	5545
(percent)	36.42	38.35	
Total	9902	5056	14958

If there were no relationship between new car ownership and gender, then both males and females would have a 37% rate. This is shown as "Observed" versus "Expected" columns for females and males, respectively, in the following table.

```
     Observed              Expected
     6296      3117        6231      3182
     3606      1939        3671      1874
```

Chi-Squared Test

The chi-squared test is based on calculating the sum of expected, minus the observed frequencies for each cell of the table. These quantities are squared to eliminate negative numbers.

Figure 3.12: Illustration of the Calculation of the Chi-Squared Test

$$\sum \frac{(o-e)^2}{E}$$

The statistic is calculated with respect to the degrees of freedom. The calculation is the number of rows (minus 1), multiplied by the number of columns (minus 1).

Degrees of freedom = (r–1) (c–1); in this case it is 1.

$$X_i^2 = \sum_{i=1,n} \frac{(o-e)^2}{E} = 5.36$$

The table is a two-dimensional table (a crosstabulation table) that shows the distribution of new car ownership within categories of gender. There are a total of 14,958 observations in this data set. A chi-squared value of 5.36 yields a probability of .02 (based on the probability table of chi-squared values). At this point, you might accept the hypothesis that there is no significant difference between males and females if you were using a .01 level of significance. If you were using a .05 level of significance, you would reject the hypothesis. In this case, gender might emerge as a significant input in a decision tree on new car ownership. If you rejected the null hypothesis, then the categories of male and female could not be merged because merging would be treating male and female categories as equivalent.

In a close case such as this, often business rules, derived from business knowledge, are used to determine whether a split is used. Alternatively, a validation sample may be used to determine whether differences between males and females persist, even if the absolute size of the difference is small.

Statistical Adjustments and the Number of Tests

As designed by Kass, the CHAID algorithm provided a method to apply statistics to assess the quality of the branches that were selected for presentation on the decision tree. Part of the statistical-testing framework included adjusting the level of significance to accommodate the number of tests of significance that were applied to determine the characteristics of a branch (statistical tests are used in forming the clusters). It is common in statistical hypothesis testing to adjust the level of significance according to the number of tests applied to a sample. This is because tables of statistical significance have been prepared assuming there is one test on one sample of data. The adjustments help prevent overfitting based on a calculation of a test statistic that is overstated.

These statistical adjustments—called Bonferroni adjustments—are designed to return a true probability level for statistical confidence that is independent of the number of statistical tests that formed the branches of the decision tree. In Figure 3.13, more statistical tests are performed with unordered categories in branch clustering than with ordered categories. Adjustments that consider the number of tests that form the branches regard either method on the same basis in terms of the values of the computed probability levels.

Figure 3.13: Illustration of Computing the Number of Statistical Tests

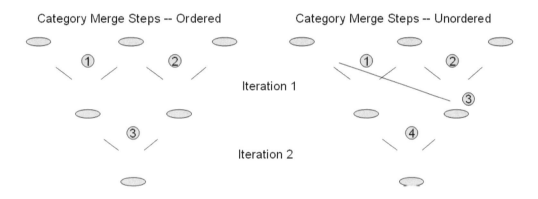

Branches are reported with a true level of significance or a worth metric; furthermore, all branches are reported on the same basis. This means that branches that consist of many values or branches that are unordered (and, therefore, can combine in many ways) are appropriately adjusted so that they can be evaluated on the same basis as a branch with fewer categories. The net result is that alternative splits are presented in a valid order in terms of their probability levels.

Research by Biggs et al. (1991) led to the development of the exhaustive method of identifying branch splits. This method incorporates Bonferroni adjustments that should be applied for the various types of inputs and number of categories that are included in the analysis. (Original work by Kass suggested Bonferroni adjustments that were more conservative than necessary.)

Other adjustments have been incorporated into the SAS Enterprise Miner decision tree. The Kass adjustment (1980) can cause the p-value to become unnecessarily more conservative than an alternative method, called Gabriel's adjustment, does. In this case, Gabriel's p-value is used.

A depth adjustment can adjust the final p-value for a partition to simultaneously accept all previous partitions used to create the current subset being partitioned. The CHAID algorithm has a Bonferroni adjustment within each node, but it does not provide a multiplicity adjustment for the number of leaves. For example, imagine an extreme case where a decision tree has grown to a thousand leaves. If a significance test were conducted in each leaf at an alpha level of 0.05, a CHAID algorithm would obtain about 50 false test of significance outcomes (reject the null hypothesis of no differences between two leaves in a decision tree). Hence, the decision tree is likely to grow too big. The depth receives a Bonferroni adjustment for the number of leaves to correct the excessive number of rejections.

In addition, there is a method to adjust the p-value for the effective number of inputs. The more inputs, the more likely an input will accidentally win over the truly predictive inputs. The more correlated inputs, the more likely the risk. The input adjustment multiplies the p-value by the number that is declared for the effective number of inputs. The default effective number of inputs equals the number of inputs that are declared live in the analysis.

An Example

Data is in the form of Amount Purchased, including Time of Purchase, Quantity Purchased, Age of Customer, and Distance Traveled. Quantity Purchased is the target field. The task is to describe the target field—**Quantity**—in terms of the other input fields.

Age	Date	Hour	Distance	Quantity	Amount	Category
35	3/21/2003	6	2	2	14.95	Shelving
29	3/21/2003	6	5	2	29.9	Shelving
40	3/21/2003	7	9	5	39.8	KitchenWare
33	3/21/2003	7	44	5	12.71	KitchenWare
50	3/21/2003	8	33	5	37.35	Shelving
27	3/21/2003	9	8	5	20	Shelving
34	11/11/2003	9	10	1	78.6	Bathrooms
58	5/17/2002	1	37	9	78.37	Bathrooms
37	5/17/2002	2	22	9	39.95	Electrical
39	5/17/2002	2	12	9	34.9	Books
24	5/17/2002	3	7	9	73	Bathrooms
44	5/17/2002	3	51	9	14.95	Bathrooms
41	5/17/2002	4	6	9	78.6	Music
30	5/17/2002	6	1	9	20	Bathrooms

With **Quantity** as a target, potential inputs include **Age**, **Date, Hour**, **Distance**, and **Category**. Total Amount could be used as an input, but would usually not be because the two measures are tightly related. In many software products, the user does not usually control the search order of inputs. In this example, the software begins by looking at the association between the target **Quantity** and the time input of **Hour**.

Some preprocessing is required before the decision tree is grown.

1. Continuous inputs need to be converted to categories.
2. The search order of inputs needs to be determined. Is the input categorical or continuous?
3. The number of allowable branches needs to be determined.
4. The similarity measure, used to combine similar categories, needs to be determined.

After this preprocessing, the target **Quantity** is set to be modeled as determined by the inputs **Age**, **Date**, **Hour**, **Distance**, and **Category**. **Hour** and **Distance** have been calculated so that the categories are meaningful. The decision tree algorithm begins by examining time, looking through such combinations as:

Hour combinations

> 9-10
> 9-10-11
> 9-10-11-12
> 9-10 vs. 11-12
> and so on

The goal of this step is to find a meaningful combination of input values that can usefully describe variations in the Quantity Purchased. This could produce a decision tree like Figure 3.14.

Figure 3.14: Illustration of a Decision Tree of Quantity Purchased Grouped by Hour

It could also be a cube-like dimensional representation like Figure 3.15.

Figure 3.15: Illustration of a Translation of Decision Tree Results to a Cube Display

As you can see, there is a direct relationship between the branches of a decision tree and the cells of a table. The notations that describe the branches of the decision tree indicate the range of acceptable values; for example, [9.5-13.5) indicates a range of values from 9.5 (including .5) 5 to, but not including, the last value before 13.5 (this is shown as 1:29 in Figure 3.15).

The decision of whether to combine values is made by a numerical or statistical test—essentially, these tests combine codes that are alike (with respect to the target), while distinguishing them from other codes.

Using the previous example, assume the next input to be evaluated is **Age**. The decision tree algorithm tries to find the best way of characterizing **Quantity** as a function of **Age**. Assume that the first age category was 14, and that the combined value for **Quantity** in the 14 age category was 5. Assuming that the next age category is 15, the decision tree algorithm essentially sets up a test of similarity between the quantities in the age category 14 compared to the quantities in the age category of 15.

The decision tree algorithm examines 14 and 15. If the two categories are similar, then the categories are combined. If age categories 14 and 15 are combined, then this combined category is compared to the distribution of target values in the age category of 16.

14+15+16   same?

If yes, combine, and so on.

14+15+16 vs. 17+18+19

Maybe the best age profile is what is shown in Figure 3.16.

Figure 3.16: Illustration of Branch Partitions Applied to a Dimensional Display

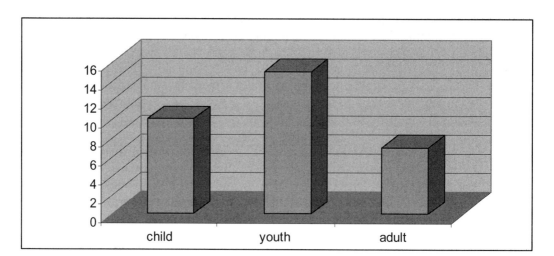

Several things are going on here:

1. This is a continuous target. If the target is categorical, the process is similar. However, the test of similarity is different. With continuous targets, the test of similarity compares variance around the average in each of the groups that are formed by the input categories. With categorical targets, a test of significance (typically, a chi-squared test) or a Gini or entropy test can be applied.
2. Multi-branch trees (i.e., more than 2 leaves) are allowed.
3. Only monotonic combinations are being looked at (i.e., combinations of a lower-valued quantity, such as 3, with a higher-valued quantity, such as 4).
4. The specifics of the test determining whether two categories are the same are not being discussed. Typically, a test of significance is used. It is possible to indicate ahead of time that you want 3-way branches or 5-way branches. In this example, the decision tree algorithm tries to split the categories into the specified number of branches to maximize the inter-branch category values and to force the greatest amount of intra-branch differences.

There are several splitting criteria. For interval targets, there are the following:

- variance reduction
- F-test

For nominal (categorical) targets, there are the following:

- Gini or entropy reduction (information gain)
- CHAID or chi-squared test

The decision trees perform the same way for the final field (**Distance**).

Figure 3.17: Illustration of Branch Partitioning for Distance

After this step is completed, the decision tree will have a candidate list of branches that could form the branches of the decision tree. If you could see inside the memory of the decision tree algorithm, you might see a table that looks like the following:

Figure 3.18: Illustration of the Candidate List for Node Partitioning

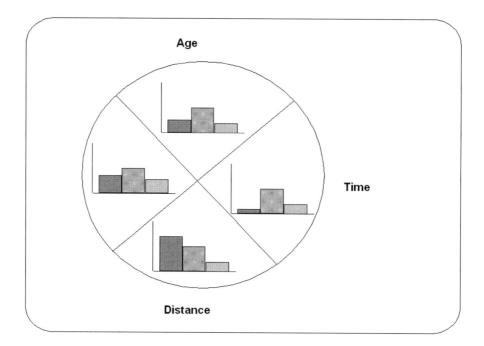

Once the values are combined, alternative branches can be compared to determine how strongly they relate to the target. This information is often used to select the appropriate branch to form the first level of the decision tree.

In the interactive mode of operation in the SAS Enterprise Miner decision tree, this candidate list of branches is displayed for selection. If you were to browse the list in interactive mode, a set of displays as shown in Figure 3.19 might be produced.

Figure 3.19: Illustration of Potential Branches in Interactive Mode

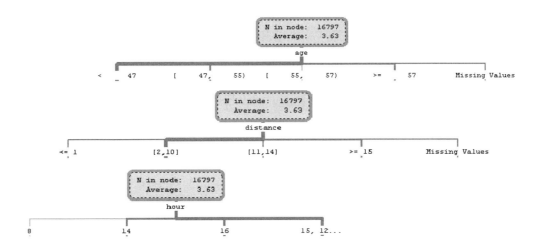

The decision tree algorithm inspects each one of these views to identify which view to choose as the splitting criterion to form the decision tree. Assume that the algorithm selected **Age** as the splitting criterion. This would produce a decision tree such as the following:

Figure 3.20: Final Branch Partition Selected at This Level of the Decision Tree

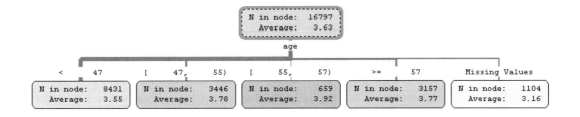

In the original CHAID algorithm, the inputs are either nominal or ordinal. Most software packages accept interval inputs and automatically group the input values into categorical ranges of discrete nominal or ordinal values before growing the decision tree. The splitting criteria are based on p-values from the F-test distribution (interval targets) or chi-squared test distribution (nominal targets). The p-values are adjusted to accommodate multiple testing. A missing value can be treated as a separate value. For nominal inputs, a missing value constitutes a new category. For ordinal inputs, a missing value can group with the code grouping it most closely resembles (as determined by a test of significance).

The search for a split on an input proceeds step by step. Initially, a node is allocated for each value of the input. Nodes are alternately merged and re-split, according to the intra-branch p-values. The original CHAID algorithm stops when no merge or re-splitting operation creates an adequate p-value. Then, the final split is adopted. A common alternative to this split method, called the exhaustive method, continues merging to a binary split, and then adopts the split with the most favorable p-value among all of the splits that the algorithm considered. After a split is adopted, its p-value is adjusted, and the input with the smallest adjusted p-value is selected as the splitting variable. If the adjusted p-value is under the threshold you specified, then the node is split. Decision tree construction ends when all of the adjusted p-values of the splitting variables in the unsplit nodes are above the user-specified threshold (because they do not meet the test of significance).

The SAS Enterprise Miner decision tree implementation is different from the original CHAID algorithm.

- CHAID transforms interval inputs into discrete categories (bins or deciles); the SAS Enterprise Miner decision tree consolidates observations into groups. In the original CHAID algorithm, these transformed interval inputs were maintained throughout the analysis. The SAS Enterprise Miner decision tree can group and regroup interval and ordinal values dynamically as the decision tree partitions data throughout the analysis.

- The decision tree node searches on a within-node sample, unlike CHAID.

The CRT Approach

In the CRT approach, it is common to grow a decision tree with more branches and sub-branches than the CHAID approach grows. The CRT approach relies on pruning to cut the branches that do not perform well. Whereas performance in CHAID is determined by a test of significance, in CRT, performance is determined by a validation approach. The CHAID approach grows decision trees with more than 2 nodes in the branches; the CRT approach grows only 2-way (binary) branches.

In CRT, branches can be selected by the following:

- **Number of Leaves.** When this selection method is used, the branch with *n* leaves (where *n* is the number of leaves selected in the user interface) is selected. Leaves refer to the number of terminal nodes on a decision tree.

- **Best Assessment Value.** This method chooses the smallest branch with the best assessment value. The assessment is based on validation data, when available.

- **The Most Leaves.** This method chooses the largest branch after pruning nodes that do not increase the assessment (based on training data).

- **Gini (CRT).** Gini is used in the CRT method. CRT uses probabilities to compute the impurity of the nodes. The formula for a node *t* is computed as:

  $i(t) = 1 - S$

  S is the sum of the squared probabilities of the components of the node. Impurity is a measure of homogeneity in the node membership for classification decision trees.

- **Variance Reduction.** This method is used to compute the best assessment value of a branch when interval data is used for the target.

For CRT, the inputs are either nominal or interval. Ordinal inputs are treated as interval inputs. The traditional splitting criteria are the following:

- for interval targets, variance reduction and least-absolute-deviation reduction

- for nominal targets, Gini and impurity

- for binary targets, Gini, Twoing, and ordered Twoing create the same splits. Twoing and ordered Twoing are used infrequently with binary targets. These criteria are considered superior to entropy or Gini criteria with multi-valued discrete targets.

The CRT method does an exhaustive search for the best binary split. Linear combination splits are also available. Using a linear combination split, an observation is assigned to the left branch when a linear combination of interval inputs is less than a specified constant. The coefficients and the constant define the split. The CRT method for searching for linear combination splits is heuristic, and might not find the best linear combination.

When creating a split, observations with a missing value in the splitting variable (or variables, in the case of linear combination) are omitted. Surrogate splits are created and used to assign observations to branches when the main splitting variable is missing. If missing values prevent the use of the main and surrogate splitting variables, then the observation is assigned to the largest branch (based on the within-node training sample).

When a node contains many training observations, a sample is used for the split search. The samples in different nodes are independent. For nominal targets, prior probabilities and misclassification costs are recognized.

The decision tree is purposefully grown to contain branches and subtrees that are not stable from the point of view of reproducibility in a new data set (or by reference to a validation data set). This intention is called overfitting. A sequence of subtrees is formed at each split. The splitting criteria are based on a measure that includes maximum-divided-by-minimum node size and the depth of the decision tree. These three measures—maximum, minimum, and depth—are used as measures of complexity. The assessment measure is calculated and used to construct each subtree. Accuracy is used as the assessment measure. If a profit matrix is available, then profitability can be used as an assessment measure. Accuracy can be computed based on a training sample, a validation data set, and a cross-validation approach.

For nominal targets, class probability decision trees are sometimes used as an alternative to classification trees. Decision trees are grown to produce discriminations between the distributions of class probabilities in the leaves. Decision trees are evaluated by the overall Gini index.

Retrospective Pruning, Cost-Complexity Pruning, and Reduced-Error Pruning

Retrospective pruning originated with cost-complexity pruning and is described in the development of the CRT algorithm by Breiman et al. (1984). This pruning method attempts to identify the best subtree. The "best" is determined by predictive accuracy, weighted by the number of leaves in the subtree. This method is a kind of "Occam's razor," meaning that the subtree with the highest accuracy and fewest leaves is chosen over any other subtree that has a similar predictive accuracy.

The decision tree in SAS Enterprise Miner provides the ability to create subtree sequences, using either the training data or validation data to compute the assessment values for choosing subtrees in the sequence. Using the training data produces a sequence that would result from using cost-complexity pruning, which was developed by Breiman et al. (1984). Using the validation data produces a sequence that would result from using reduced-error pruning, as described by Quinlan (1987). Reduced-error pruning relies exclusively on validation data; it finds the subtree that is best for a validation data set and does not rely on the creation of sequences of subtrees.

Selecting the Final Branch

The decision of which branch to select to form the split is an important one because the form of the subsequent decision tree depends entirely on which branch, with which number of nodes or leaves, is selected. Following are some of the main considerations:

- Select the branch that will develop the best descriptive model for the analysis.
- Select the branch that will develop the best predictive model for the analysis.
- Select the branch that will develop the best explanatory model for the analysis.

If the goal is to construct a descriptive model, then it is best to create splits in branches that reflect the business user's conceptual approach to the subject area. In this case, the strength of a split on a decision tree is less important than the form of a branch. For example, if states are split into regional groups that reflect the business structure of the enterprise, the description is enhanced. This could be a preferable split over one which yields a better predictive result, but is less intuitive.

When prediction is the goal, the form and shape of the decision tree might never be examined at all. In this case, you want good predictive results. This is measured by the validated prediction or classification rate of the decision tree. The result can be visually inspected using indicators such as a lift chart.

When the goal is explanation, it is useful to grow the branches of the decision tree in a particular sequence. This enables you to construct a decision tree where earlier effects are introduced higher in the decision tree. Therefore, their effects on lower or later effects can be gauged. Sequencing can be used to suggest the form of the interactions among inputs with respect to the target. This is a way of using the decision tree to support explanations that relate to presumed sequences of events and interrelationships. This treatment is not usually possible if the decision tree is grown for simply descriptive purposes or for maximizing prediction.

Step 6—Complete the Form and Content of the Final Decision Tree

After the first level of the decision tree is formed, the decision tree algorithm can be applied recursively to the nodes (or, at this point, leaves) of the first branch. These nodes become candidates for splitting into branches, in the same way as the original root node was examined. This process continues recursively until a full decision tree is grown. The process can be stopped in a number of ways, as discussed below.

It is worthwhile to stop at a good point to avoid overfitting the decision tree. Detecting overfitting is important because:

- If the decision tree is overfitting the data, then the relationships that are displayed in the decision tree are not stable and could be a source of misunderstanding about the relationships in the data.

- If the decision tree is overfitting the data, then predictions, which are based on the structure of relationships as identified in the decision tree, will not be good. This means that the predictive power and reproducibility of the decision tree will be weak.

Stop, Grow, Prune, or Iterate

Statistical measures and validation methods can be used to decide how large to grow a decision tree and to evaluate the quality of the decision tree.

After the branch has been selected to form the first level of the decision tree (which is below the root node), the process of splitting is repeated for each of the leaf nodes in the new decision tree to fill out the decision tree to its final form.

The process of forming the CHAID decision tree continues until a node is selected that cannot produce any significant splits below it. Or, the process continues until a stopping rule is encountered. A typical stopping rule might be: "Do not split any node with less than 10 records in it" or "Do not create any node with less than 10 records in it".

The process of forming the CRT decision tree begins much like the CHAID process. CRT forms binary decision trees, rather than multi-way decision trees. While CHAID uses adjusted tests of significance to stop tree growth, CRT relies on validation tests to prune branches, to stop tree growth, and to form an optimal decision tree.

In CHAID, after a node is split, the newly created nodes are considered for splitting. This recursive process ends when no further node can be split. The reasons a node can no longer split are the following:

- The user can decide when to stop.

- The node contains too few observations to split in a meaningful way.

- The maximum depth of the decision tree (i.e., the number of nodes in the path between the root node and the given node) exceeds a specific level (typically set by the user).

- No split exceeds the threshold worth requirement specified in the F-test or chi-squared significance level value, or in the variance reduction setting.

The last reason is the most informative. Typically, in this situation all the observations in the node contain almost the same target value, or no input in the node is sufficiently predictive. The decision tree approach is very effective at developing a strong fit between the branches of a decision tree and the data that is used to discover the particular form of the decision tree. However, this type of use comes at a price. The specific form of the decision tree, particularly at lower levels, cannot be exactly reproduced when applied to new data. Decision trees that fit the training data at deeper levels often predict too poorly to apply to new data. While the general form of the higher-level branches might track new data well, lower-level branches are more idiosyncratic and cannot usually reproduce in new data.

When the basic defaults for growing the decision tree are set to extreme values, the decision tree is likely to grow until all observations in a leaf contain the same target value. Such decision trees overfit the training data and will poorly predict new data.

A primary consideration when developing a decision tree for prediction is deciding how large to grow the decision tree or what nodes to prune. The CHAID method specifies a significance level of a chi-squared test to stop tree growth. The originators of the C5 and CRT methods argue that the right thresholds for stopping tree growth are not knowable in advance, they recommend growing a decision tree too large and then pruning nodes.

The SAS Enterprise Miner decision tree node provides both the CHAID approach and the grow-and-prune approach. A sequence of subtrees of the original decision tree is always grown—one subtree for each possible number of leaves. After the sequence of subtrees is established, the decision tree node uses one of four methods to select which subtree to use for prediction:

1. most leaves
2. at most indicated number of leaves
3. best assessment value
4. average profit

The user typically determines the desired subtree method. Options available include:

- if at most indicated number of leaves = *n* subtree (*n* is the number of leaves in the subtree)
- best assessment value

If the first approach is selected, then the decision engine uses the largest subtree with at most **n** leaves. If the second approach is selected, then the decision engine uses the smallest subtree with the best assessment value.

The decision tree stops growing at a certain point, depending on the outcome of this assessment. The assessment is based on the validation data when available. If the subtree method is set to **most leaves**, then the node uses the largest subtree after pruning nodes that do not increase the assessment. For nominal targets, the largest subtree in the sequence might be much smaller than the original unpruned tree because a splitting rule can have a good branch assessment value (split worth) without increasing the number of observations correctly classified.

Assessment Measures

The most common assessment measure is proportion correctly classified if the target is qualitative or categorical, and the sum of squared errors if the target is quantitative. For continuous targets, average square error is used.

Other assessment measures include proportion of event in the top 50% on target 1. This uses the half of the observations that are predicted most likely to equal 1, and uses the training data to compute the proportion in which the target equals 1. This measure can be extended to include proportion of event in the top *x*% on target value *y*. This uses a user-defined threshold as an alternative to 50% to observe the successful classification rates at an arbitrary percent level (for example, 33 to compute the percentage of success in the top third).

In summary, the CHAID method does the following:

- performs subprocess 2–4 in the selected node, for all nodes
- stops when no more branches are significant
- stops when cell sizes fall below a certain threshold (or when nodes of a certain size cannot be produced)

The CRT method picks the best subtree for each of the extremities of the decision tree through pruning. The final decision tree is the tree that is left after the subtrees have been pruned according to the tree growth selections.

Key Differences between CHAID and CRT

The main difference between a CHAID approach to growing a tree and a CRT approach lies in whether a test of significance or a train-and-test measurement comparison is used.

In the classical CHAID approach, a test of significance forms the groups of codes that form the branch. In turn, this branch is evaluated with a test of significance to determine whether it is used in the decision tree. In the CRT approach, a number of methods can be used to form the branches (although, classically, a variance reduction approach is used to form binary branches). The resulting branches are tested against a validation sample to determine whether the branch accuracy is sufficiently high enough to be used in the decision tree.

Accuracy can be computed many ways. In the simplest way, a decision tree is grown and the predicted classification or prediction is tested against the data set used to train the form of the decision tree. This is called a resubstitution test. The predicted score is substituted for the original score in the training data set, and the overall accuracy rate is computed by comparing the substituted score with the original score.

The resubstituted accuracy rate appears higher than the true accuracy rate because the same data that is used to train the form of the decision tree is used to test the efficacy of the form that was trained. Training the form of the decision tree in this way might pick up idiosyncrasies in the training data that are specific only to the training data This means that the data is not reflective of the data universe that the training data is designed to reflect. So, the trained decision tree contains these idiosyncrasies. The accuracy rate is computed on training data that includes the idiosyncrasies because this is the same data that was used to train the decision tree.

If a new data set from the data universe was used to test the accuracy of the decision tree, it is unlikely that the new data would include the idiosyncrasies that the trained data included. The accuracy rate that would be computed with this new data is less than the accuracy rate that would be computed using resubstitution.

One-pass resubstitution always overstates accuracy rate. Multi-pass methods, such as cross-validation or boosting through re-sampling, produce better results. A better, more accurate rate would come from the use of a new, independent data set. This is the preferred method of computing the accuracy rate. This means that a separate data set is made from the original data and is used for testing purposes only. Because it is made before the testing begins, this data is not likely to have idiosyncrasies that will be trained in the decision tree.

Guiding Tree Growth with Costs and Benefits in the Target

When there is a gain and loss associated with correct and incorrect predictive decisions, it is important to incorporate cost and benefit into the selection of decision tree targets. A cost or profit can be assigned to an outcome. The implied profitability of a recommended outcome (the prediction) is used to determine the final form of the decision tree. Psychologists have shown that implied costs and benefits lie behind a wide range of human decision-making. This theory is based on the theory of signal detection (Green and Swets). For example, the decision of whether you have enough gas to get to the next gas station when driving on a road carries a different weight than the decision of whether you have enough gas to get to the next airport when flying a jetliner. On the road, the implied saving of time might easily outweigh the potential cost of running out of gas before arrival; this is not so on the jetliner. Timeliness is important, but easily offset by the potential cost associated with a catastrophic loss of life. Moreover, different decision-makers (as well as their decision-making tools) make different decisions based on their decision-making style (for example, whether they tend to be conservative or more liberal).

Guidance in decision-making tasks is provided by referring to a confusion matrix, as shown in Figure 3.21. The event of interest—**X**—can either occur or not occur. So, it is either **X** or **Not X**. The confusion matrix compares the actual distribution of **X** and **Not X** to the observed (or predicted) distribution. Hits happen when the predicted event—**X**—actually occurs. Misses happen when, for example, it is predicted that there is an **X** event, but, in actuality, it is **Not X**.

Figure 3.21: Confusion Matrix

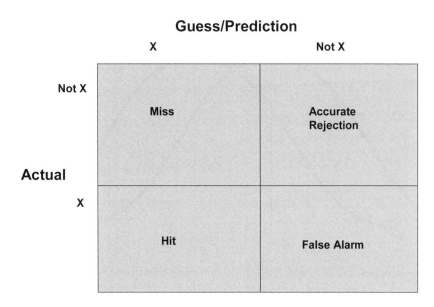

Signal detection assesses the effectiveness of the decision boundary that is used to determine whether an event is **X** or **Not X**. The idea of signal detection is shown in Figure 3.22. There are two distributions—A and B. Distribution A represents the distribution of an outcome; for example, the probability that a customer who buys a pair of jeans will also buy an accompanying sweatshirt. Distribution B represents the same distribution with noise or uncertainty added. This noise comes from a variety of sources, such as a conservative versus liberal decision-making style. The difference between the two distributions is illustrated by the line showing the distance between the peaks of the two distributions.

Figure 3.22: Illustration of Signal Versus Noise Distributions in Signal Detection

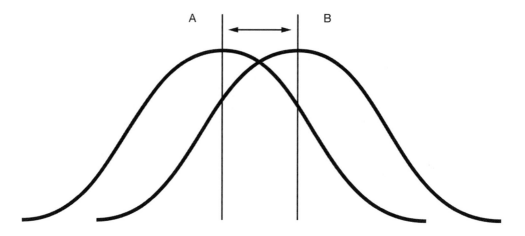

The signal detection theory says that, given the uncertainty represented by the difference between the two distributions, decisions can result in hits, misses, false alarms, and correct rejections. If you guess that the customer will buy and the actual result is a purchase, then you have a hit. If you guess that the customer will buy, but the customer does not buy, then you have a false alarm. If the customer buys and you guess that the customer will not buy, then you have a miss. One goal of signal detection is to determine the ideal circumstances that maximize correct decisions (hits and correct rejections), while minimizing incorrect decisions (misses or false alarms).

This can be illustrated by referencing the area under the distributions in Figure 3.23. You see the effect of a default 50% decision threshold that represents a halfway point between conservative and liberal. The area to the right of the threshold represents hits, and the area to the left represents misses.

Figure 3.23: Illustration of the Effect of Decision Threshold on the Signal Versus Noise Distributions

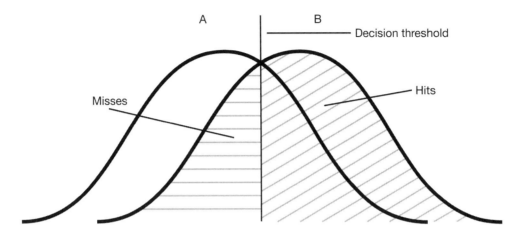

Costs and benefits can be used to construct predictive decision trees that are accurate (regardless of the decision method) and produce the most profitable result. This is possible because decision thresholds are rarely clear-cut and can be changed to reflect costs and benefits.

Figure 3.24: Illustration of Hit Rate Given the Decision Threshold on the Signal Versus Noise Distributions

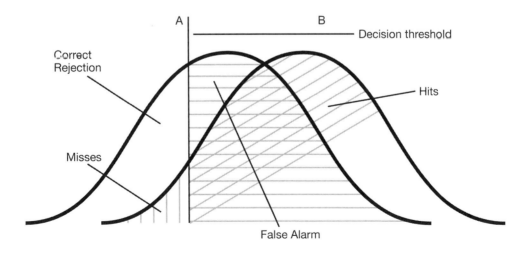

Other Software Features

As shown in Figure 3.25, a change in the decision threshold can change the proportions of hits, misses, and false alarms. When comparing Figure 3.23 to Figure 3.24, you see that while hits increase and misses decrease, there is an accompanying increase in false alarms.

This situation is shown in Figure 3.25. A grid is set up to compare the distribution of values that are predicted by the decision engine at a given threshold. If you predict the presence of an event—designated with **X**—then you have a hit. If there are events in the data, but you do not predict them, then you have a miss. Similarly, when you predict an event, but the event is not there, you have a false alarm.

Figure 3.25: Illustration of Hits and Misses at a 50% Decision Threshold

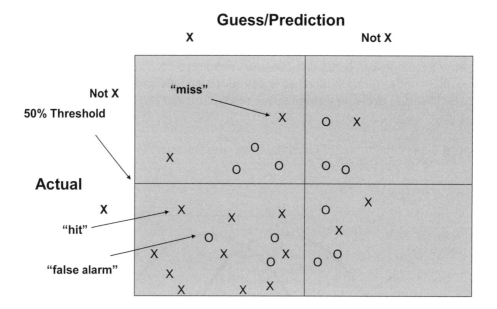

Figure 3.25 shows the distribution of a target value in a record (illustrated as **X**) and whether the value is detected at a baseline threshold. For illustration, assume that the decision threshold is 50% - a common setting for most decision-making tasks. This threshold reflects the notion that if the probability of an event, as estimated by the prediction engine, is .5 or greater, then you will set the decision to the event (in this case, **X**). If the probability is less than .5, then you will set the decision to **Not X**. A results table, called a misclassification table, is shown below. There are 15 **X** events in the prediction space and the prediction engine has correctly identified 10 of them. This provides a sensitivity of about 67%. This sensitivity was gained from a decision threshold of 50%, that returned 13 predicted **X** events overall. The success rate of this prediction engine is 10 out of 13—77%. This is called the specificity.

Table 3.2: Misclassification Table

Predicted	Actual		
	x	*not-x*	*sum*
not-x	5	9	14
x	10	3	13
sum	15	12	27

If you assigned a benefit or return metric to a hit, and assigned a penalty or cost to run the prediction engine, then you would see that a good prediction engine maximizes sensitivity and specificity. Assume that a hit is worth $20 and that the cost per candidate to run the prediction engine is $5. In this example, this means that the return was $200 and the search cost was $65.

Now, consider changing the decision threshold to 65%. In this example, demand a predicted probability of .65 or greater before you predict that an event is present in the data records being classified. This might produce a result as shown in Figure 3.26.

Figure 3.26: Illustration of Hits and Misses at a 65% Decision Threshold

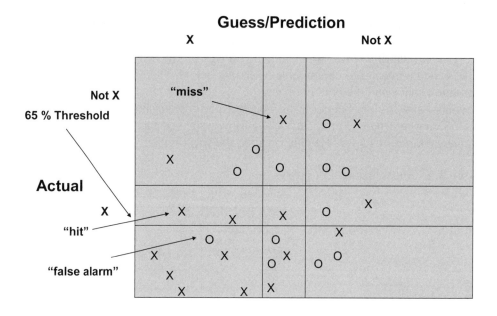

If you look at the return on investment of this decision approach, you see that there were 12 hits (for a return of $240) and that the search cost was $115.

	Actual		
		not-	
Predicted	x	x	sum
not-x	3	1	4
x	12	11	23
sum	15	12	27

Now, look at the two approaches, as shown in the following table:

	50% Threshold	65% Threshold
Sensitivity	0.67	0.80
Specificity	0.77	0.52
Return on Investment	200	125

If you use the typical 50% cutoff in estimating the probability of an event (for example, an additional purchase), then you will get x hits. You also get y misses. Now, if you shift the decision threshold to a 65% cutoff, then you increase the number of hits to $x+1$. The misses decrease, but, as expected, the number of false alarms increases.

Prior Probabilities

Prior probabilities for the target classes can determine whether the counts and proportions in the formula for the assessment measure are adjusted by prior probabilities. For example, suppose 60% of the observations have a target value of 0, and the remaining 40% have a target value of 1. Assume that the decision tree predicts all observations to be 0, and the prior probability of 0 is 10%. Because the decision tree predicts all zeros, then it appears that the misclassification rate is 40% (because the apparent distribution shows 40%). If prior probabilities are incorporated in the assessment measure, then the proportion misclassified would be 90%. Otherwise, it would be 40%.

Figure 3.27: Illustration of the Effect of Prior Probabilities on Apparent and Real Distributions

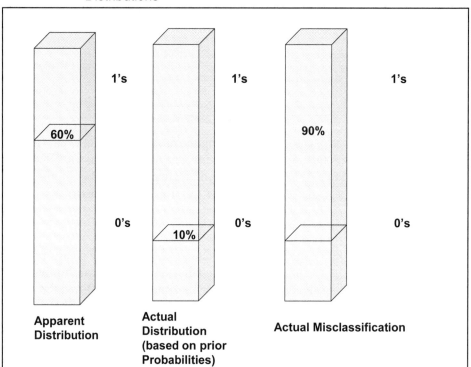

Prior probabilities do not change the shape of the decision tree. The decision tree makes the same prediction, regardless of whether the assessment measure incorporates prior probabilities or not. Only the assessment results change with the prior probability specification.

The decision tree always uses prior probabilities when predicting a target value. If the training and validation data sets are obtained by oversampling observations that have a rare target value, then incorporating prior probabilities in the misclassification rate could offset the goal of oversampling, which would artificially boost the apparent incidence of a rare code in the training data. On the other hand, when the assessment measure is the proportion of the event in the data, then the incorporation of prior probabilities would give a better idea of how the decision tree will perform when it is deployed in a live environment with new data.

Business Intelligence and Decision Trees

Introduction

Business Intelligence (BI) applications have been one of the fastest growing applications in the early years of the twenty-first century. BI applications provide a set of tools and techniques to enable the storage, retrieval, manipulation, and display of data to domain experts and business analysts in a form that facilitates business and policy decision-making. BI applications are part of a maturity evolution in the computer industry that has enabled the use of computers to move from operational applications that can be used to run the business, to analytical applications that can be used to drive the business and steer its direction.

A key feature of BI is the deployment of a wide range of readily available reporting capabilities. Deployment is achieved without obvious intervention of specialized IT staff. The consumers of the information contained in the reports have a much higher degree of access than was possible before the development of BI. As a result, BI has become a pervasive business tool and approach since its origin in the mid-1990s.

Key drivers of BI use include:

- the development of data warehousing concepts and techniques (to access data and to combine multiple data sources to form a view of data that can be consumed by BI computer agents)

- the development of data and dimensional storage and retrieval capabilities that have been adapted to serve in the BI reporting engines

- the evolution of a wide variety of data viewing techniques, including the production of reports, spreadsheets, business graphics, and Web deployment environments

More recently, BI has given rise to the identification of business analytics. The term "business analytics" explicitly recognizes that there is so much data available and that there are so many factors involved in business processes and business decision-making that analytical approaches and techniques are a necessary underpinning for BI to perform effective data summarization and trend identification. In the beginning of BI, its analytic nature and the real-time deployment of results to the user led to a description of the area as OLAP (Online Analytical Processing). The term "OLAP," which is still used, has given way to "multidimensional cubes" and so provides a broader description of the area.

Traditional BI tools enable an analyst or decision-maker to display multiple views of multiple items of interest. For example, BI reports and spreadsheets show sales by region, sales by time, or sales by product line. With the increasing incorporation of business analytics within the BI framework, there are more methods and mechanisms to use business analytics in the identification, explanation, and dissemination of BI results.

For example, many views can be derived from the following display:

Credit-Worthiness	Mortgage Due	Home Value	Length of Residence	Age
1	25860	39025	10.5	64
1	70053	68400	7	21
1	13500	16700	4	49
0	97800	112000	3	60
1	30548	40320	9	31
1	48649	57037	5	47
1	28502	43034	11	38
1	32700	46740	3	42
1	20627	29800	11	28
1	45000	55000	3	36
0	64536	87400	2.5	47
1	71000	83850	8	40
1	24280	34687		31
1	90957	102600	7	23
1	28192	40150	4.5	54
0	102370	120953	2	45
1	37626	46200	3	62
1	50000	73395	5	
1	28000	40800	12	67
1	17180			56
1	34863	47471	12	34

This display can be viewed as cube slices, as shown in Figure 4.1.

Figure 4.1: Illustration of Cube Slices Defined for BI Display

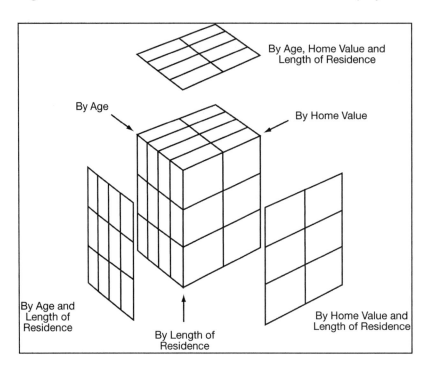

When viewed this way, you can see that the cube concept is dominant in BI. Many advances have been made in both the front end (data presentation) and back end (data warehousing, data integration, and data manipulation) aspects of BI to handle the range of records, fields, field values, and associated observations, variables, and variable values that are richly reflected in the enterprise data store. BI products are timelier, more accessible, and more flexible than ever before.

As the state of the art continues to evolve, there has been a corresponding demand in the area of business analytics. Improvements in techniques in the areas required to perform prospective tasks in BI are needed:

- Provide multi-factor versus single-factor approaches and displays. Until recently, it was common to show 2-way diagrams (e.g., sales by region) or 3-way diagrams (e.g., sales by region by product line). The ability to show multi-factor hot spots and soft spots has been difficult to produce (for example, produce a display that shows that while sales in the west for new products are low, this is not the case for special segments of the population).

- Provide forward-looking, predictive, or what-if approaches versus historical, snapshot-of-the-past approaches.

The tasks of understanding and identifying business drivers require classifying and confirming trends and relationships in the data. Multidimensional cube tools and regression perform these tasks. Multidimensional cubes form the underpinnings of BI. Cubes or multidimensional cube tools enable business users to look at multiple views of their business data as they seek a better understanding of the trends and relationships that are relevant to their business. Cubes provide pre-calculated and pre-summarized dimensions of information, which results in instantaneous retrieval and examination. The ultimate goal is to better understand the data-based drivers of the business so that these drivers can be anticipated and manipulated in ways that are favorable to the business.

Whereas multidimensional cube tools are based on pre-calculated dimensions to improve a user's judgment when assessing trends and relationships, multivariable techniques, such as decision trees and regression, are based on statistical knowledge and business experience in order to generate results on the fly. Multidimensional cube tools and regression can explore the classification and predictive power of multiple fields of data in a data store. Cubes are limited by their reliance on pre-calculated fields; simply put, not all relevant business dimensions can be pre-calculated and pre-summarized in a business analysis. There are significant limits to a user's judgment and cognitive abilities in terms of the number of quantities that can be judged and manipulated, as well as in the reliability and accuracy of size estimates, when exploring and comparing various effects in the BI display. Decision trees are well adapted to producing results that can be rendered as cubes for reporting purposes.

A Decision Tree Approach to Cube Construction

Like BI tools, decision trees perform the tasks of trend and pattern identification. Decision trees are built using a methodology that explicitly addresses the need to identify the relationships between the factors that combine to provide a complete view of the area being examined. Decision trees are designed to search for a wider range of relationships than multidimensional cubes or standard regression methods. Because decision trees drill down to the record level in data, they enable multidimensional business reports that identify trends and patterns that might be missed in normal, multidimensional cube and regression analyses that rely on aggregate data.

The BI report is based on displaying facts (usually from the fact table of the underlying data warehouse) along preselected dimensions and sub-dimensions. BI reports are defined ahead of time to reflect commonly used business reporting dimensions. Decision trees also display facts (usually from the distribution of a target field) along dimensions and sub-dimensions, which are formed by the branches of the decision tree. The major difference between the dimensions of a decision tree and the dimensions of a BI approach is that the dimensions of a decision tree are formed on an ad hoc basis, either automatically or through user interaction. Decision tree displays result from compressing or collapsing dimensional values on the display. Values of the dimensions and sub-dimensions are collapsed to show similarities and differences among the dimensional values that are not highlighted in BI displays.

Decision trees evolved as data analysis tools in both applied and academic settings. The earliest use of decision trees was in a marketing research analysis that involved an audience. Other early uses were developed to assist the identification of relationships in data to support sociological and economic research at the Survey Research Center at the University of Michigan. Decision trees have had a strong business analysis orientation from the early days of their conception.

Decision trees began as a method of finding tables within tables or relationships within relationships. In this respect, they are like multidimensional cube tools in that they both look at various dimensions of data and within a dimension, they both look within sub-dimensions. As decision trees matured, the goals extended to handle continuous and categorical table cell entries and multi-way branches. Statistical tests and validation approaches were developed to assure the integrity of the decision tree. Decision trees use data search and summarization algorithms and verification and validation mechanisms that distinguish them from multidimensional cube tools.

Multidimensional Cubes and Decision Trees Compared: A Small Business Example

Assume you have a lemonade stand and are selling lemonade by the glass or by the jug. You have a database of sales transactions. You even have a number of fields of information where you collect additional data each time you make a sale.

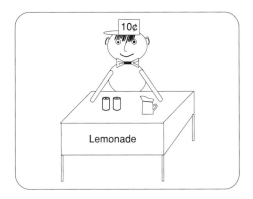

A sales transaction record might appear as follows:

Sale Item	Quantity	Price	Discount	Time of Day	Sales Agent	Customer Identifier

You use the database to calculate sales commissions and to keep track of inventory to reorder supplies. Today, with the growth of analytical systems, you could use this data to try to understand your customers and your sales patterns, to create sales campaigns, and to drive new product development. You could look for types of sales that maximize the profit from your sales effort (ROI).

A typical multidimensional cube analysis starts with historical business queries and reports. It attempts to identify dimensions in the data that elaborate the business model to create views of the contextual effects. These views lead to a better understanding of the relevant business issues. The multidimensional cube analysis proceeds intuitively—it follows hunches to look for relationships that can be used to better understand or predict events. Consider your database of lemonade sales to determine sales trends.

A multidimensional cube analysis might look at sales by time of day, as shown in Figure 4.2.

Figure 4.2: Illustration of a Multidimensional Cube by Time of Day

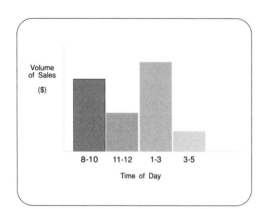

Or, the analysis might characterize customer by customer type.

Figure 4.3: Illustration of Age Characteristics of Customers

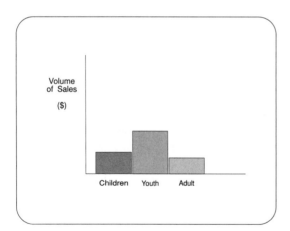

Or, the analysis might break down sales by volume.

Figure 4.4: Illustration of Sales by Volume

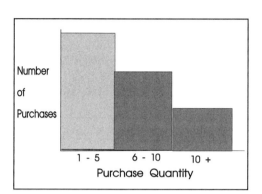

The analysis might even look at sales by geographic area served (customer origin).

Figure 4.5: Illustration of Customer Origin

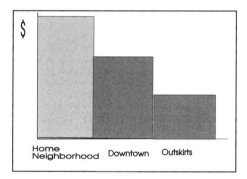

Behind the scenes, a typical multidimensional cube analysis is based on a cube that has dimensions of analysis that have been determined as being important characterizations of the business data. Following in Figure 4.6 are two simple examples—one in two-dimensional form and one in three-dimensional form.

Figure 4.6: Multidimensional Cube Analysis

Customer	$						$				
Quantity	$					$	$		$		
Location	$				$	$	$	$	$	$	$
Time of day	$	$		$	$	$	$	$	$	$	$	$	$	$	$

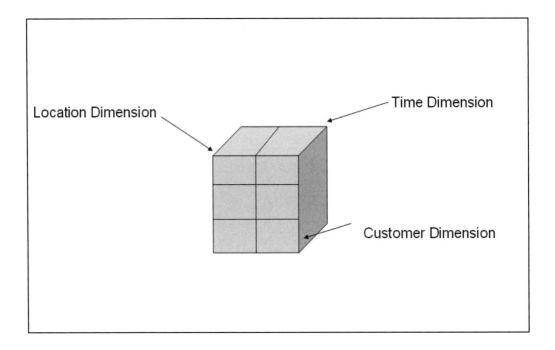

In these examples, the business user is using the cube definitions and associated data tables to present views of the data. Views could be a screen display or a printed report with graphics. Figure 4.6 shows 2-way relationships: one field on one axis, and one field on the other axis. However, multi-way relationships are possible and desirable. The ability to drill down into various views of data and show multi-way relationships within a dimension enables multidimensional cube tools to show one or more relationships in the context of another relationship; for example, a multidimensional cube tool can show the discount rate for a product for an enterprise division.

Although both decision trees and multidimensional cube tools show multi-way relationships in context, there are important differences between the two; multidimensional cube tools do not have the same relationship-searching capabilities that decision trees have, nor do they have the onboard statistics or validation facilities that decision trees have. A decision tree looks through more relationships than a multidimensional cube looks through; furthermore, a decision tree verifies and validates relationships as being statistically or numerically sound.

Multidimensional cube views are designed to support quick viewing and decision-making by the business user. As a result, the cubes are built to optimize the user's time. Much care and effort are required in constructing the underlying multidimensional cube database and in precomputing the contents of the views, sub-views, and drill-downs that the business user is likely to review. This means that the business user is not able to point and click through various alternative analysis scenarios within the multidimensional cube environment, as can be done with decision trees.

Because the dimensions of a cube analysis are created from a preexisting warehouse and because the associated reports are often pre-calculated, multidimensional cube reports tend to be more structured and rigid than decision tree reports. For example, typical state aggregations can be drawn along regional lines—East, West, South West, and so on. These dimensions can be fixed by business rules and business policies. Nevertheless, once the dimensions are established and set up either in the data warehouse or as reporting dimensions in the multidimensional cube reporting application, they cannot easily be changed, nor can they be recombined based on a relationship in the data (for example, combine all high-margin states).

Decision trees permit the recalculation of dimensional groupings on the fly. They support dimensional groupings that are based on the properties of data and the relationships between data elements, rather than on business rules or business policies. For example, the following decision tree shows how trees can be used to form the framework of a cube.

Figure 4.7: Illustration of a Decision Tree as Raw Material for Cube Construction

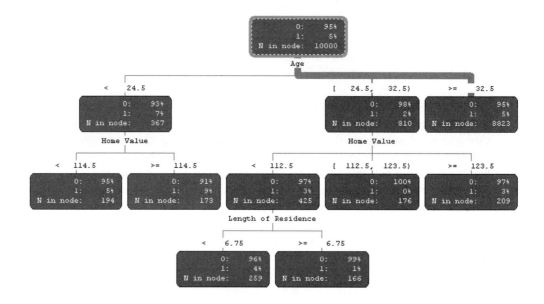

Decision trees provide utilities to tell you which variables are important and which interactions (i.e., which cube faces and cube combinations) should be presented. From Figure 4.7, you can see many useful features for the display of cubes.

The decision tree identifies empirical-based ranges of values to collapse (or group) within display fields, such as age. Normally, these ranges are predetermined or calculated mechanically. The decision tree identifies whether sub-dimensions are significant (from a statistical point of view, and also from a business-rules perspective) and, if so, what the optimal collapsed categories for the values should be.

In Figure 4.7, you can see that at the top level of the decision tree, the optimal code ranges for **Age** are < **24.5**, **24.5** to **32.5**, and >= **32.5**. The structure of the decision tree suggests that two sub-dimensions, based on **Home Value**, are appropriate in the lower **Age** range. **Length of Residence** is an appropriate sub-dimension in the low-end value of the middle **Age** range.

Multidimensional Cubes and Decision Trees: A Side-By-Side Comparison

Multidimensional cubes and decision trees can be compared and contrasted as follows:

- While multidimensional cubes have pre-built data dimensions, the dimensions of decision trees are dynamically collapsed to highlight similarities and differences among and between nodes that are being formed by the decision trees. These nodes are equivalent to classes in the cells of the tables.

- In decision trees, the dimensions and groupings can be determined by business rules, as BI approaches are, but they are more commonly determined by the strength of the association or prediction, which is based on numerical methods or statistical approaches. Typically, the dimensions and groupings are formed through a dynamic that combines business rules with numerical methods and statistical approaches.

- Multidimensional cubes are almost always retrospective; that is, they show what has already happened based on the data. Decision trees are retrospective, prospective, and predictive. Like multidimensional cubes, decision trees show how the data is arranged in-line with the historical past. Decision trees can be used to extrapolate and infer future events. Underlying rules are commonly used as the basis for predictive and expert systems.

- Decision trees are more effective at handling missing values. Missing values are handled by using surrogate or stand-in values or by treating missing values as a different code that is grouped with similar codes in the reporting dimension of the decision tree.

Table 4.1: Comparison of Multidimensional Cubes and Decision Trees

Multidimensional Cube	Decision Tree
Shows tabular views of data as tables with relatively fixed dimensions; dimensions are determined primarily on the basis of business rules	Shows tabular views of data within relevant dimensions as determined by computational algorithms and business rules
Has database that is pre-built to support anticipated queries	Has database that is pre-built to support numerous unanticipated queries
Provides quick view retrieval	Has lengthy retrieval
Tends to limit number of cross-views or relevant factors	Has few limitations on the relevant factors
Makes it difficult, almost impossible to identify novel results	Emphasizes novel results and the identification of important versus unimportant contributions

Decision tree results can be made to look very much like multidimensional cube results; the branches of a decision tree are just simple n-way tables that show the relationship between the attributes of the field that is used to form the branch and the values of the target in that node or leaf. Like multidimensional cube tools, decision trees can display both categorical and continuous n-way relationships in any node or leaf. Like multidimensional cube tools, a leaf is presented in the context of higher-level dimensions. In a decision tree, these higher-level dimensions are the higher-level branches. In a multidimensional cube, the higher-level dimensions represent the drill-down sequence that was followed to be at that face in the cube.

Both decision trees and multidimensional cube tools provide a drill-through capability (i.e., the ability to display and analyze detailed information that belongs to the individual records that characterize the relationships that are displayed in any single table, leaf, or face of the cube). And, just as decision trees can be represented as multidimensional cubes and associated displays, multidimensional cubes can be represented as decision trees (although typically, they are not).

Both multidimensional cubes and decision trees provide the means to apply all relevant dimensions when identifying key drivers that affect a target or outcome value. However, multidimensional cube dimensions are displayed and examined hierarchically, whereas decision trees present results in tree form as a network. In summary, both support a style of analysis that can lead to identifying important relationships between fields or variables that need to be considered to accurately and reliably describe and predict a target or outcome.

Multidimensional cubes present numerical results (such as average, standard deviation, mode, range, and count) within the cells that are formed by the dimensional categories. Decision trees can present numerical values and categorical values as the target.

The Main Difference between Decision Trees and Multidimensional Cubes

The major difference between decision trees and multidimensional cubes is the heavy concentration of statistical and search algorithms that are built into decision trees. All forms of multidimensional cube analyses depend on the creation of a view of the analysis data. The view enables the dimensions of the cube to be retrieved and assembled as the various faces of the cube are selected for analysis and display. In this respect, decision trees require less preprocessing of the data and of associated dimensions because the statistical and search algorithms have been built to identify the specific form of dimensions at the time that the decision tree is grown.

Decision trees support a looser initial definition of the dimensions of data that are included in the analysis. They support a more dynamic identification of the specific structure of the dimensional relationships through the use of the statistical and search algorithms. These algorithms assemble the dimension in real time as the decision tree is grown.

The actual statistical and search algorithms in decision trees are another major difference between decision trees and multidimensional cubes. Decision trees provide more methods to identify the strength of relationships than are provided in multidimensional cubes. Furthermore, decision trees provide more methods to guard against overfitting the data (i.e., decision trees provide methods to identify inaccurate and unreliable relationships, which is not usually provided in multidimensional cubes).

Overall, decision trees can uncover more relationships and more effects—based on unique groupings—than multidimensional cubes can. In addition, decision trees provide more options to check the efficacy of relationships that are discovered and displayed, which helps prevent overfitted relationships and the misunderstandings and unreliable predictions that are associated with them. Some multidimensional cube tools provide forecasting or predictive features, but they do not provide as many options and validation functions as decision trees provide.

Regression as a Business Tool

The use of regression techniques has long been a mainstay in scientific research and statistical process control. The pervasiveness of computers and information technology in business environments has created a situation that is ripe for uncovering uses for regression in business data analysis. Although regression is used in relatively specialized areas such as supply chain management, statistical process control, and database marketing, it has not been adopted as a business intelligence tool, even though it would address the major prescriptive requirements for BI approaches to provide forward-looking multiple-indicator results. The same could be said about more recent techniques, such as neural networks. Neural networks could serve as a flexible family of nonlinear regression and discriminant analysis techniques. They are in the same class of methods as regression techniques.

Although the multidimensional cube is the most prevalent type of data analysis tool used in business settings, regression is used very often. And while the multidimensional cube is a recent data analysis tool, regression has been used in business and scientific settings for many decades.

Regression describes the relationship between two quantities in the form of an equation where one quantity—Y—is viewed as a function of the other quantity—X. This simple relationship can be shown as follows:

Figure 4.8: Illustration of a Typical Regression Result

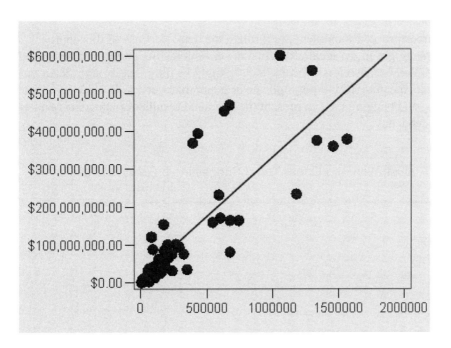

In this simple case of regression, the relationship is approximately linear. The regression method has been extended in many ways. For example, the target—**Y**—can be a function of multiple predictors. The form of the relationship has been extended so that both linear and nonlinear relationships can be included. And, in addition to numeric quantities, nonnumeric qualitative information (i.e., categorical data) can be included.

Decision Trees and Regression Compared

Decision trees and regression share a common form where target values are associated with multiple input values in order to show the form of the association and to be able to predict new target values based of new input values. Although regression and decision trees perform the same function, which is displaying a relationship between a target (outcome or response) variable and one or more input variables, they take widely different approaches. Regression works by manipulating an entire matrix of information that contains all the values of all the inputs against the target and that attempts to compute an optimal form of the relationship that holds across the entire data set.

Decision trees proceed incrementally through the data. Because of this approach, a decision tree might find a local effect that is very interesting and would be missed by regression. Yet, because it is a local effect, it might be only locally significant or locally reproducible, meaning it will not replicate or generalize very well. New approaches, such as boosting and bagging (which present the averaged results of many decision trees), offset this tendency.

Figure 4.9 Illustration of a Linear Trend Suggesting a Good Regression Fit

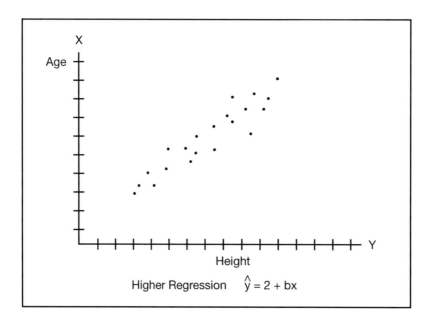

Regression is capable of presenting a linear relationship, as shown in Figure 4.9. A simple relationship can be eloquently expressed as a linear equation. Decision trees can only approximate this relationship, as shown in Figure 4.10.

Figure 4.10: Illustration of Decision Trees Displaying a Linear Trend

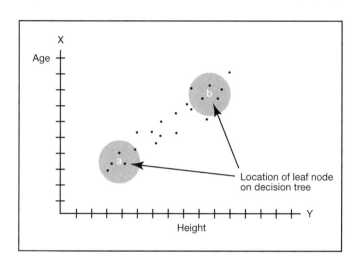

When trying to reproduce a linear relationship with decision trees, various parts of the linear relationship are fit by many components of the decision tree. This produces a staircase-type of relationship fit, as shown in Figure 4.11.

Figure 4.11: Illustration of the Staircase Effect When Multiple Decision Trees Fit a Linear Trend

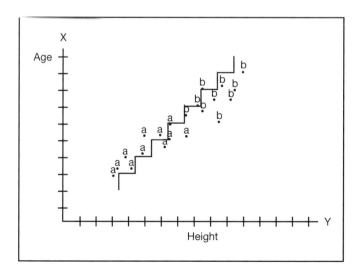

Under certain circumstances, this staircase effect can be useful, for example, when the audience has difficulty conceptualizing the regression equation. Or, this effect can be more visual when the branches on the staircase represent convenient and well-understood conceptual categories (e.g., child, preadolescent, adolescent, young adult, and so on). Often, a decision tree reveals just enough of the necessary information to be easily and intuitively interpreted, as shown in Figure 4.12.

Figure 4.12: Illustration of an Intuitive Decision Tree Displaying a Fitted Linear Trend

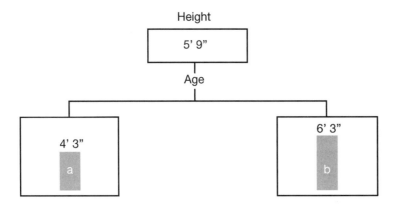

New approaches that handle many decision trees at once (e.g., boosting and bagging) offer a method of producing a smooth surface like you see with regression.

Differences between Regression and Decision Trees

The differences between regression and decision trees, as well as the indicators of the strengths and weaknesses, can be described as the following:

- local versus global search
- rules versus coefficients
- distributional and metric assumptions about the data
- description of the relationships

Local versus Global Search Decision trees attempt to find a function that can split the observations of a target (outcome or response) into subgroups that form descendent branches. These subgroups are candidates for further splitting until some stopping criterion is met. When a decision tree processes a data set, it does so in successive increments where each increment produces a leaf node that becomes a local subset where the relationship between the response and the input variables is described in a local context.

On the other hand, regression attempts to find a function that can characterize the observations of a target (outcome or response) so that the deviations between the score of the function and the actual function are minimized across all cases. The regression approach manipulates the data set and the input variables that it contains as a single canonical representation. While decision trees proceed one branch at a time to identify combined effects, regression identifies combined effects of all inputs simultaneously and then identifies individual effects. More differentiated functions are introduced into the regression equation to construct an optimal deviation-reduction function. The regression approach is global in contrast to the local segments of decision trees.

Rules versus Coefficients Decision trees proceed to segment data on an incremental basis by descending to lower branches of the decision tree. Unlike regression, decision trees look at each input separately and iteratively. They recursively choose between alternative groups or branches of input values to grow the decision tree by splitting nodes in-line with groups or branches that are identified.

By comparison, regression techniques are holistic. Regression identifies the combined and individual effects of data on the basis of matrix operations that capture and summarize the relationships between inputs and target as a single multidimensional expression. While decision tree results can be described as a series of incremental <IF> <THEN> rules, regression results are described as a series of coefficients for the model inputs. These coefficients are computed with respect to the values of all other coefficients that are in the model.

The regression equivalent of a node can be conceptualized as a slope. The value of the slope is captured by the coefficient bx in the following expression:

$$\hat{y} = 2 + bx$$

This expression reveals the upward trend in the distribution of x-y points in the regression line, as shown in Figure 4.8.

In their simplest forms, decision trees and regression equations perform different and complementary functions.

- A decision tree provides a graphical representation of the structure of the relationships in data. The decision tree identifies how the target rises and falls as the data that is associated with the target is filtered through views provided by the multidimensional breakdowns represented as leaves in the decision tree.

- A regression equation provides a clear and mathematically rigorous expression of the form of the relationships in data that is reflected by the sign and strength of the coefficients in the regression equation.

Decision trees were originally developed as a complement or alternative to linear regression. One of the earliest decision tree implementations of AID was used to detect nonlinear effects and interactions among predictors in a regression equation. Decision trees readily select sub-segment effects in a data set that might be missed by regression.

Decision trees deliver their sub-segment effects through their recursive partitioning method. This offers the advantage of more readily selecting sub-segment effects, but it does so at the cost of requiring much data to work with. As decision trees successively partition the data set, smaller sub-segments of data are created at lower levels of the branches of the decision tree. Because regression computes the combined effects of all data points through a summary operation that works with all data points simultaneously, regression does not dice the data in the same way decision trees do and it makes more efficient use of the available data. Neural networks, like decision trees, readily select nonlinear and sub-segment effects that are contained in the data.

Distributional and Metric Assumptions About the Data   A major difference between decision trees and regression is the use of categorical or nonmetric data values. This difference underscores a general difference between decision trees and regression that relates to the assumed form of the data that underlies the approaches. Because decision trees successively segment input values based on discrete, nonmetric distinctions, decision trees work with data that can be measured in a variety of metric and nonmetric (quantitative and qualitative) ways. On the other hand, regression is a quantitative technique based on an approach to data manipulation that assumes that data values are linear and additive. Common intervals are inferred so that the metric distance between values 10 and 11 is the same as the metric distance between values 11 and 12, and so on. The statistical techniques at the core of the regression algorithm rely on data that is distributed according to the law of large numbers. When data deviates from this form, the regression technique begins to break down. Although there are techniques for handling deviations, the results become more uncertain and more difficult to produce.

Description of the Relationships As decision trees and regression have evolved, there has been an increasing cross-fertilization of techniques drawn from these two approaches. For example, regression approaches now accommodate nonlinear relationships and interactive effects in data. A common way to accommodate nonlinear relationships in a regression equation is to form a variable that is used to segment the data set so that different regression equations are fitted for different subsets of data. In this way, nonlinear effects are isolated by different regression equations that are formed for the different subsets. Decision trees can be used to construct the variable that is used to segment the data set. This is one of the many preprocessing functions that a decision tree can do before a regression analysis. SAS Enterprise Miner provides facilities to do this.

Likewise, decision trees have evolved to include simple and multiple linear relationships as splitting criteria in the construction of a decision tree. Decision trees can now apply fine-grained layers of branch partitions that are computed through resampling. As a result, the data space is cut into finer discriminations that resemble the discriminations made by regression equations. The differences between decision trees and regression have become smaller over the years.

Over time, hybrid approaches have evolved. A decision tree can be used as a preprocessor for regression to identify one or more atomic leaf nodes that, in turn, can become outcome groups to be modeled in the context of a regression analysis. By the same token, error-reducing functions, developed in the regression modeling framework, can be used to identify the attributes of the branches that should be used when creating the decision tree.

Because decision trees are developed recursively, they result in successively finer subcategories of data and successively smaller subgroups. Each subgroup is uniquely defined by the sequence of multidimensional branches that must be scanned to define the subgroup. These are the attributes of the subgroup that distinguish it and separate it from the other subgroups in the data. Unfortunately, as the decision tree grows deeper, it is harder to comprehend the overall view of data that the decision tree is describing. For this reason, decision trees that are more than three layers deep can be hard to understand. Also, as the decision tree deepens, branches are identified and displayed that rely on fewer observations to determine their characteristics. As a result, the reliability, accuracy, and reproducibility of the decision tree are threatened by the fewer observations that are used to shape the decision tree.

Regression techniques share a similar fate. Regression equations do not artificially divide the data into finer subcategories; however, they divide the data into finer functional descriptions. Ultimately, this means that regression equations suffer from opacity and a complexity of interpretation that decision trees do not suffer from. With decision trees, each and every subgroup can be precisely, easily, and uniquely defined through a visual or automated scanning of the decision tree or the rule representation.

Theoretical Issues in the Decision Tree Growing Process

Introduction

The discussion in previous chapters has served to highlight and illustrate the two major characteristics and attractions of decision trees as methods of dealing with data:

- to extract and apply information from data, particularly predictive information

- to extract and communicate insight from data

The first major characteristic, prediction, emphasizes the accuracy and reproducibility of the decision tree model and does not emphasize the underlying form, structure, or intrinsic comprehensibility of the decision tree. The second major characteristic emphasizes pattern detection, identification, and communication. This approach is exploratory and can be used as a precursor to other techniques, such as multidimensional cube reporting or building predictive components.

The strength of decision trees for exposition is in the decision tree's ability to uncover multiple effects both visually and intuitively. To create the best decision tree for expository value, the decision tree often takes a form that maximizes expository efficacy, but might compromise or undermine the decision tree's optimal numerical powers in prediction and accuracy. There can be a trade-off between the business-rules approach to decision tree use and the statistical efficacy.

Since the initial substantial deployment of decision trees as data analytical tools in the '70s and '80s, decision trees have solved many of the early problems that labeled them as ineffective prediction tools in terms of validity, accuracy, and efficacy. Recently, encouraging developments have suggested that predictive goals and descriptive insight goals are not necessarily antagonistic. Results presented by Breiman in the area of random forests (2001) and Friedman in gradient boosting (1999) demonstrate the effective communication of what seems to be deeply complex, potentially obscure multi-tree models. Both random forests and gradient boosting are boosting approaches that resample the analysis data set numerous times to generate results that form a weighted average of the resampled data set. When summarized, the results of many decision trees are better than the results of a single decision tree. In both random forests and gradient boosting, the emphasis is not so much on detecting the form and representation of a single decision tree, but on presenting a graphical representation of the associated decision tree predictive components, such as scores and deviations.

Whether the goal is prediction or insight, a major benefit of decision trees is exposing relationships and patterns in data, generating predictive results, and communicating these findings. The user's task is to understand the various approaches and to choose wisely when conducting analyses.

Crafting the Decision Tree Structure for Insight and Exposition

Growing a decision tree for insight (extracting conceptually appealing information from data) and exposition (displaying the decision tree results in a form to communicate insight and to inform policy and planning) needs to be fully understood. The goals of insight and exposition differ and complement the goal of using decision trees to extract key relationships and predictive structure from data (which satisfies the requirement of maintaining an overall form, structure, and sequence of branch formation in the decision tree). The decision tree reveals information and communicates best when it can be used to "tell a story" that fits the conceptual framework of the audience. The story illuminates key interests and potentially contains a few plot twists that upset conventional ways of looking at the data and, hence, pave the way for the development of insight and improved understanding.

In telling the story, it is important to have a beginning, middle, and end. The story should be told in terms that are familiar to the audience. And, while it can be useful to include a few twists in the plot, the insights that are revealed should be plausible. The best way to ensure a good story line is to construct the decision tree in-line with the conceptual model of the area that the decision tree is designed to illuminate. For example, if you are looking at purchase behavior, then the attributes of the decision tree need to reflect concepts that are relevant to purchasing behavior. If the application is quality control and you are looking at part failures, then the attributes of the decision tree need to reflect concepts that are relevant to part failures.

Every application area in which expository decision trees can be deployed is characterized by concepts that either explicitly or implicitly exist in the minds of the audience. Concepts have been measured and reflected by different entities in the data set and can be linked differently, particularly if the entities suggest different links based on the empirical characteristics of the data. However, there is always an underlying story line, a presumed relation, and a presumed cause and effect or sequence of causes and effects. Some decision trees can be more comprehensive than others. One characteristic of a comprehensive decision tree is that the data in the conceptual area that is being explored contains a range of related attributes. As a result, the story that is told by the decision tree reflects both a plausible set of relationships and a fairly complete set of relationships (i.e., to the extent possible, the substantial drivers of the relationships being explored have been included).

To build this type of decision tree for exposition, the following tasks should be performed:

1. Determine the conceptual model.
2. Determine the data measures, fields, and field values that will become the operational components of the conceptual model when the model is translated to form the decision tree.
3. Develop the story line (i.e., the presumed sequence of events as the operational components unfold to tell the story).
4. Determine key relationships or potential plot twists to be examined in shaping the form of the decision tree.

Conceptual Model

So far, the decision tree concept has been described by the analogy of telling a story. It can also be described by comparing it to the traditional scientific method. In the scientific method, you begin with a theoretical model. From the theoretical model, you build an exposition that consists of an operational model. Then, you form constructs that reflect empirical data and that can develop a set of hypothesized relationships and proposed tests of hypothesis that can demonstrate the mirroring between the operational model and the theoretical model.

While the decision tree is constructed to be readily consumed and useful to the audience, it is also constructed to support scientific rigor and defensibility on scientific and engineering grounds. This kind of defensibility is essential because ultimately, the decision tree results are designed to become enterprise policy deployments that will produce substantial savings and profits. Therefore, no matter how appealing the story is or how compelling the plot is, the results must be scientifically robust to support a review and implementation program that could offer significant benefits.

A decision tree can illustrate the operation of the model being used to explain the relationship being examined. The most important consideration relates to crafting the structure and sequence of the branch partitions used to expose the model and explain the results, in explanatory modeling or when you want to expose the relationships between the multiple factors in the model and the target.

Consider the following weather forecasting example:

Figure 5.1: Illustration of a Conceptual Model of the Analysis of Weather Patterns

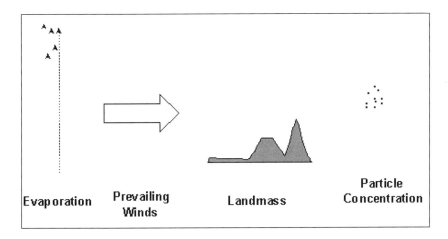

A simplified model of weather might be as follows—water evaporates over the ocean, forming clouds of moisture in the air. These clouds move in a direction based on the prevailing winds. Moisture can be squeezed out of the atmosphere depending on what happens to the prevailing winds as they encounter landmasses. Finally, if there are particles of dust in the air, the condensation of water droplets to produce rain is accelerated.

The prediction of rain or shine depends on the cumulative operation of a sequence of variables. The winds have no effect unless there is evaporation for them to carry. Landmasses and particle concentrations on their own cannot produce rain; they need the winds that carry moisture. And, without landmasses and particle concentrations to run into, moisture could be carried by the winds forever and never be released.

If there is rain and a mountain range nearby (a frequent event on the West Coast of North America), you should not conclude that the mountainous surroundings have produced the rain. This is an example of a spurious relationship. To know the whole story, you need to measure evaporation over the ocean, you need to measure the speed and direction of the prevailing winds, and so on.

When growing the decision tree so that it will reflect this order in the model of the domain, you should observe this sequence of events. There are many competing branches at the top level of a decision tree. It is common to have a number of alternative branches—all significantly related to the target (as indicated by their logworth measure). The question becomes, "Which branch should I select?" For the purpose of exposition, it is best to select branches in the order that conforms to your modeling framework. This usually involves selecting a branch with a lower logworth than other available branches. In the weather example, this suggests that the topmost branches of the decision tree should reflect evaporation rate. Next, you should select branches reflecting the operation of the wind. Then, you should select branches reflecting landmass profiles and particle concentrations, in that order. In some cases, you might select a branch that does not pass a test of significance. It is important to include these nonsignificant branches in the displayed decision tree so that the conceptual model is properly reflected.

These tasks can be called the analytical approach or the analytical framework. They are illustrated in Figure 5.2.

Figure 5.2: Illustration of the Top-Down Work Breakdown to Develop an Analytical Model

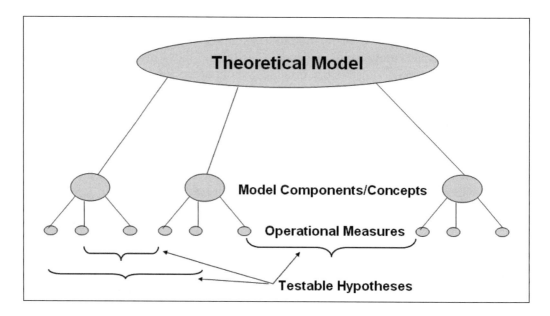

In the purchasing example developed in Chapter 2, the theoretical model could presume that purchase preference follows socioeconomic status and is influenced by life cycle factors, such as marital status, home ownership, and children. Other influential factors can be presumed, such as sociopsychological lifestyle and personal preference. A predisposing factor, such as a recent loan or home purchase, might be a signal that indicates an immediate or impending change in one or more of the dimensions of life cycle. To better understand, consider the balloon-and-line diagram in Figure 5.3.

The balloons can illustrate the components of the model. The connecting lines can illustrate the presumed relationships. To model the relationships in the form of a decision tree, you need data that encapsulates the presumed behavior of the components in relationship with one another. The data is used to derive the empirical measures that will operationalize the behavior that you want to examine.

As the model evolves, you can form hypotheses to test as you construct the decision tree that represents the conceptual approach. After forming the hypotheses, you can control and guide the construction of the decision tree. This, in turn, puts you in a position to meaningfully, constructively, and efficiently produce and interpret the results that you find.

Figure 5.3: Illustration of an Analytical Model

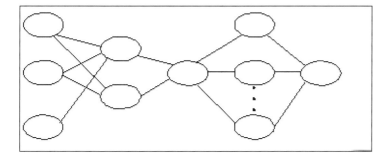

Following is an example hypothesis:

Is there a limit to the variety of drinkable products a consumer will be attracted to? How is this limit distributed in my current (and future) market population? How will this vary over time and by customer?

Question 1:   How can various products be clearly packaged and differentiated?

Question 2:   Which of these product packages can give me a satisfactory ROI given the competitive environment and satisfactory marketing mix (product, price, place, promotion)?

Each layer in the model can consist of theoretical constructs that are operationalized by the database contents. Operationalize is the process of assigning numeric tokens for conceptual entities. For example:

Table 5.1: Theoretical Constructs

Socioeconomic Factors	Sociopsychological Factors	Psychological Style	Range of Preferences	Buying Decisions
Age Education Marital/Family Status Income	Marital/Family Type of Employment Indebtedness	Outward-Directed versus Inward-Directed	Outdoor Products Indoor Products	Buy Product X Buy Product Y

The hypothesis is that the propensity to buy the explosive, multi-fruit blend is a function of adolescent, upwardly mobile, outdoor-oriented, outward-looking types, with elevated levels of spending power.

To support the evolution of the plot as the story unfolds while building the decision tree, you must introduce the branch partitions in the order that is implied in the conceptual model shown in Figure 5.4. The top branches of the decision tree are grown to reflect the background socioeconomic factors. Next, sociopsychological factors and psychological style factors are introduced. Finally, the range of preferences are introduced (if available). Preferences provide the most accurate and attention-grabbing presentation of the combination of factors and relationships that are optimal in capturing the data in the context of extracting meaning to understand purchase behavior.

This method of growing the decision tree can correctly preserve sequence information and explicit and implicit time-ordered relationships in the data so that the results reflect the logic of preconditions and consequent targets. Simpson's paradox states that if you are examining relationships among the independent variables, then the sequence of the construction of these variables can be important. There are limits to computation-based measures; this is an opportunity for the analyst to rely on knowledge of theory, practice, and experience to choose the branches and sequence of branches in the decision tree. Furthermore, in a data mining context, it is common for a data set to have hundreds of potential inputs serving as explanatory or descriptive decision tree components. It is not sufficient to let the decision tree grow in a way in which branches are picked on the basis of predictive strength. To explain the results, it is important to construct the form and sequence of the branches. A heuristic approach that is based on the underlying conceptual model can substantially reduce the construction burden on the analyst.

A practical method is to use a fishbone or Ishikawa diagram. In the retailer data first discussed in Chapter 1, you can start with an Ishikawa diagram as shown in Figure 5.4.

Figure 5.4: Illustration of an Ishikawa Diagram to Organize the Constructs of an Analytical Model

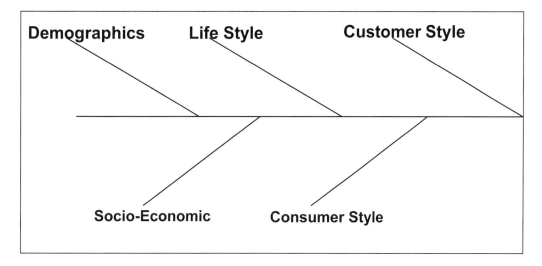

In practice, determine what dimensions are likely to be relevant by examining the source data. The source data is shown in the following display.

Number	Variable	Dimension
1	gender	Demographic
2	occupation	Socioeconomic
3	owns_truck	Lifestyle
4	owns_motorcycle	Lifestyle
5	owns_RV	Lifestyle
6	valueOfCar	Socioeconomic
7	length_of_residence	Socioeconomic
8	maritalStatus	Demographic
9	age	Demographic
10	hasBankCard	Consumer Style
11	hasStoreCard	Consumer Style
12	has_card	Consumer Style
13	has_credit_card	Consumer Style
14	has_upscale_store_card	Socioeconomic
15	children_home	Lifestyle
16	adultsInHH	Lifestyle
17	income	Socioeconomic
18	has_new_car	Socioeconomic
19	Recency	Customer Style
20	lifeTransactions	Customer Style
21	lifeVisits	Customer Style
22	NetSalesLife	Customer Style
23	state	Demographic
24	bathroomPurchases	Customer Style
25	bedroom	Customer Style
26	kitchen	Customer Style
27	juvenile	Customer Style
28	table	Customer Style
29	windowDisplay	Customer Style
30	couponPurchase	Customer Style
31	Monetary Value	Customer Style
32	Frequency	Customer Style

There are a number of potential inputs for the five dimensions, as shown in Table 5.2.

Table 5.2: Measurement Inputs

Dimension	Measures (Inputs)
Demographic	4
Socioeconomic	6
Lifestyle	5
Consumer Style	4
Customer Style	13

There are numerous potential combinations of branches if all measures for all dimensions are inserted into the decision tree. By constraining the order of entry, the potential number of combinations is reduced considerably. This might be considered a shortcoming if the only goal in growing the decision tree is predictive accuracy. However, it is damaging beyond repair if the goal is to grow a decision tree that can be displayed and explained in conceptual terms that are relevant for an audience that is eager to better understand its business or research.

In summary, remember that data represents operational measures of concepts or of analytical constructs. For example, atmospheric pressure is a concept. The height of a column of mercury is used as a method of making the concept operational. As the mercury rises, the atmospheric pressure diminishes. In all the models, data is used as an operational measure of some analytical construct. The characteristics of the phenomenon being modeled can be captured and exposed by examining the relationships between the data points that operationalize the various terms in the construct. To maintain the time-ordered nature of effects and produce a more readily interpretable decision tree, you should introduce branches with fields that move from the left to the right in the causal sequence of effects (as you move from the top to the bottom of the decision tree).

Predictive Issues: Accuracy, Reliability, Reproducibility, and Performance

Decision trees are sensitive to the sequence of branch growth. Once a branch is selected, it affects the structure of the entire decision tree below it. Thus, is critical to be very careful in selecting the sequence of branches that are introduced into the decision tree if the goal is to interpret the decision tree components to gain a better understanding of the factors that influence the area under examination.

If the goal is raw prediction, then the sequences of chains of branches in the decision tree in terms of their expository value are less important. What is important is identifying sequences that have predictive value. In this situation, decision tree quality relates to how well the decision tree performs in terms of accuracy, reliability, and reproducibility. Because some computations can be time-consuming, quality also relates to the ability of the decision tree to deliver results within defined time periods. A number of techniques are available to capture these various dimensions of quality.

Sample Design, Data Efficacy, and Operational Measure Construction

Sample Design. The issue of sample design applies to all situations where empirical data is used to gain knowledge of the environment. The data that is used to gain knowledge of the environment must be representative of the environment. For example, with lemonade stand sales, you assume that the data is representative of the situation that you are modeling. There are random elements in data collection. For example, different people pass the lemonade stand on different days; thus, the data collected depends on the day that the data was collected.

The variability and potential gaps in data can affect the results produced in the decision tree. Suppose lemonade sales are modeled on either time of day (morning versus afternoon) or on location (corner versus mid-block). On some days, such as hot days, time of day might best explain sales. On other days, location would predict better. If data were collected over several days, including both hot and not-so-hot days, the time model and the location model might predict sales with about the same degree of accuracy.

For prediction, either model will produce good results. However, for explanatory purposes, the models might suggest completely different things. One model might suggest selling only in the afternoons, saving the cost of morning operations. The other model might suggest paying more for a corner location. It might turn out that an underlying variable—in this case, temperature—would explain both the time of day and the location differences, but because of the variability in data collection, this variable is missing from the data.

Data Efficacy and Operational Measures. In addition to constructing a comprehensive data sample, it is important that the data contains information that relates to factors that are known to be or likely to be relevant to understanding and predicting the target. So, if temperature is relevant, then you need to have measurements of temperature.

It is also important to have true metrics to reflect measures. Cold, warm, and hot might not be as good as temperature measured by a thermometer when building the effects of temperature into the model. Many measurements of human behavior do not follow a linear form. As amply illustrated by extensive work in psychometrics, most forms of human perception are not only nonlinear, but are often non-monotonic and circular in nature.

Strong Sets of Predictors. After sample design, data efficacy, and measuring, the most likely issue to emerge in growing the decision tree for prediction involves identifying strong sets of predictors. A predictor is strong if it is consistently and accurately related to the target or outcome under examination. In a previous example, height and weight were generally good combined predictors of gender. In a decision tree framework, you want to identify ranges of height as nodes in a decision tree that have an associated likelihood of predicting male or female gender. The same is true of weight and height-weight combinations.

The difficulty with decision trees is selecting ranges that work well. A range of 90–110 pounds in one sample can be almost exclusively female. Yet, in another sample, this range can be 50% females and 50% males. The challenge is to find not only strong predictors, but also strong ranges or cut-points in the branches of the decision trees. This is the rule, rather than the exception. This is especially true in regression when some of the input variables are associated or collinear. Some variables at cut-points can suppress the effects that might otherwise be observed at lower parts of the decision tree. An unstable model often provides reliable accuracy, but without reliable explanation.

Another challenge is to find strong combinations of predictors (i.e., height-weight combinations that produce consistent predictions of gender over time). Tree-based models are particularly unstable. Small changes in the training data can completely change the structure of the decision tree. If the variable in the first splitting rule changes and another branch is substituted, then the descendent branches can be very different.

The two most generally applied approaches to identify predictor combinations in decision trees rely on statistical tests of significance, usually with multiple Bonferroni adjustments and various forms of validation or cross-validation.

There are many options to deal with instability in the inputs that are selected:

- use stand-in variables (i.e., a variable that approximates the unstable variable, but is more reliably related to the outcome)
- create composites (e.g., principal components or factor scores or another reduction measure that is more stable because it represents the weighted combination of multiple indicators)
- get more data to capture more power in the relationships that are being examined

A best-fit model is neither too big nor too small. At some point in the growth of the decision tree, after one or two top predictors have been identified, you might be tempted to introduce another predictor. For example, in the height and weight data, you might want to use age to capture another dimension of the predictive space and, consequently, produce a more accurate or reliable prediction.

How large should the final decision tree be? The interpretability of the decision tree decreases as you descend to its lower levels. And, the statistical power of the results is weakened. The developers of the CRT approach have done the most work in this area. The CRT approach grows an overly large decision tree and then prunes.

As shown in Figure 5.5, there is a point of divergence between the readings provided by a training data set and the readings provided by a test data set. At the point where the trained form of the decision tree model is not replicated in an independent sample, it is time to prune the decision tree.

Figure 5.5: Illustration of the Drop in Accuracy in Training and Test Data with Complexity

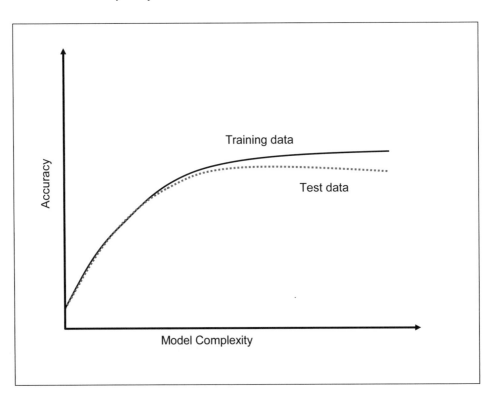

Choosing the Right Number of Branches

If the goal is predictive, then there are rare cases in which an unordered, multi-way split can create better predictive results than a binary decision tree. If you have strong theoretical reasons for presenting an unordered grouping of codes in predetermined (or computed) clusters, then you should. You might even get superior predictive results.

If the goal is explanatory, there is no statistical answer, per se. You can use experience or theoretical reasons to assist you in creating multi-way groupings that are logical or that concisely capture the nature of the subpopulation. This will help you interpret and communicate the results. It will enable you to find more meaningful interactions among the predictors. If you have reasons for a binary decision tree (e.g., North-South, East-West), then use one. If you have reasons for a multi-way decision tree (e.g., East-Mid-West-West), then use it.

Multiple Decision Trees

The traditional form of a decision tree model works with a single target variable that is predicted based on a collection of inputs. Typically, this target is modeled as a function of the values of an associated row of inputs. The model is built across the entire data set and uses all or most of the rows of data as the learning or training data set. Often, one or more data sets are taken as a random sample from the original data set. This data is used to test or validate the model that is developed.

To score a data set with a single decision tree, the records of the data set are run through the rule set that has been produced by the final decision tree of the modeling phase. This process is true for any target value, whether it is continuous or categorical. Typically, many single decision tree models are built by the analyst. They are evaluated by inspection or by reference to the test or validation data. One or more preferred decision tree models are selected as the product of the modeling phase.

The process of vetting various decision trees supports the original concept of developing formal methods of multiple decision tree modeling. In these methods, the original data set is used to create derived data sets or alternative decision tree models. These data sets or models are used to develop multiple decision tree models and scoring algorithms. One or more of the derived data sets can be used as test or validation data. Scoring is performed by pooling the results of the multiple decision trees that are grown. These pooled results can be compared to the results of a panel of experts. As in real life, the results from a panel of experts outperform the results of a single expert.

A single decision tree can produce the following results:

```
IF Age > 20
AND Weight > 180 (lbs.)
THEN Gender = Male
```

Multiple decision trees can produce the following results:

```
Rule 1

IF Age > 20
AND Weight > 180 (lbs.)
THEN Probability of Gender = Male is .6


Rule 2

IF Height > 160 (cm.)
AND BodyMass < .3
THEN Probability of Gender = Female is .3
```

The results can be pooled using various voting algorithms. For example:

```
Target Assignment = .6(Rule 1) + .4(Rule 2)
```

The combined probability of **Male** is (.6 x .6) + (.4 x .7), which is .36 + .28. This equals .64 and because this is greater than .5 (equal probability), the outcome is male. Many voting algorithms have been devised to assess the combined outcome, just as many voting algorithms have been devised to determine committee votes in real life. Different voting algorithms can be devised and used depending on the circumstance. Using multiple rule sets to derive a summary score is sometimes called an expert committee.

Advantages of Multiple Decision Trees

One of the main problems of a single decision tree model is that small changes in the data set can produce substantial changes in the model. Thus, small changes can easily change the size and shape of a decision tree. There is a tendency to overfit the data and it can be difficult to determine the most appropriate size of a decision tree. These small changes in the composition of the data can influence which branches are grown or pruned in a decision tree.

In medical diagnoses, it is common to ask for a second opinion. Even though the diagnosis is coming from an expert in the field, this expert might have idiosyncrasies that could bias the outcome of the medical examination. Similarly, a single decision tree might reflect idiosyncrasies that could bias the predicted results.

One solution to these two problems is to grow multiple decision trees using a randomization approach and then combine the information from the multiple decision trees into one summary representation. This approach was initially developed in the mid-1980s as a form of cross-validation.

In this approach, instead of relying on a single decision tree, many decision trees are assembled to create an aggregate outcome that represents the summary of all decision trees. The approach repeats and reinforces an argument made by Surowiecki in his book *The Wisdom of Crowds: Why the Many Are Smarter Than the Few and How Collective Wisdom Shapes Business, Economies, Societies and Nations* (2004). He relates the story of an observation made by Francis Galton at the 1906 West of England Fat Stock and Poultry Exhibition. As many as 800 people, both experts and nonexperts, participated in a contest to guess the weight of one of the showcase oxen. The guess had to be based on the weight after the ox had been slaughtered and dressed. While no one person guessed the correct weight, which was 1,198 pounds, amazingly the average of the 800 odd guesses was 1,197 pounds!

Since the initial development of the multiple decision tree approach, numerous research studies and practical results have demonstrated that aggregation based on multiple decision trees significantly improves model results. Because many models are developed and averaged, the results are highly stable. The traditional form of the decision tree display cannot usually be produced using multiple decision tree methods, but other forms of display are available and as effective as the simple single decision tree display.

Major Multiple Decision Tree Methods

The major methods for multiple decision tree modeling include cross-validation, v-fold cross-validation, and bootstrap-based methods (i.e., boosting and bagging (bootstrap aggregation)). Bootstrapping is useful as an estimation technique and in drawing multiple samples from a host data set as input to multiple decision tree learning environments. Recent innovations include arcing, adaptive gradient boosting, and random forests.

Cross-Validation

A method of multiple decision tree modeling was introduced in the mid-1990s with the use of cross-validation in the CRT decision tree approach that was developed by Breiman, Friedman, Olshen, and Stone. All of the rows in the learning data set are used to build the initial decision tree. This parent decision tree is allowed to grow larger than normal because cross-validation is then used to trim branches. The parent data set is partitioned into groups called folds. Typically, 10 folds are used; this is called 10-fold cross-validation. Nine of the partitions are used as a new cross-validation training data set. The 10% (1 out of 10 partitions) of the data that was held back from the cross-validation training data set is used as an independent test sample for the test decision tree. This data is run through the test decision tree and the classification error rate for that data is computed. This error rate is stored as the independent test error rate for the first test decision tree.

A different set of nine partitions is now collected into a cross-validation training data set. The partition held back this time is different from the partition held back for the first test decision tree. A second test decision tree is built and its classification error rate is computed. This process is repeated 10 times, building 10 separate test decision trees. In each case, 90% of the data is used to build a test decision tree, and 10% is held back for independent testing. A different 10% is held back for each test decision tree. Once the 10 test decision trees have been built, their classification error rates (which is a function of decision tree size) are averaged. This averaged error rate for a decision tree size is known as the cross-validation cost.

The decision tree size is a function of how many terminal nodes or leaves exists on the decision tree. Two different sized decision trees might yield the same cross-validation cost. The cross-validation cost for each size of the test decision tree is computed. The decision tree size that produces the minimum cross-validation cost is found. The parent decision tree is pruned to the number of nodes matching the size that produces the minimum cross-validation cost. The pruning is done stepwise, removing the least important nodes during each pruning cycle. The decision of which node is the least important is based on the cost-complexity measure, as described in *Classification and Regression Trees* by Breiman et al. Cost complexity exploits the notion of parsimony; i.e., every thing equal, a simpler model is preferred to a more complex model. Thus, cost-complexity pruning penalizes branches that are lower on the decision tree.

Note that cross-validation is different from the split-sample or hold-out method. In the split-sample method, only a single subset (the validation data set) is used to estimate the generalized error rate, instead of k different subsets (i.e., there is no cross folding).

Cross-validation and bootstrapping both use resampling to estimate generalized error rates (Weiss and Kulikowski 1991). The resulting estimates of generalized error rates are often used when choosing a model.

Bootstrapping

During the 1990s, the method of bootstrapping gained currency and wide acceptance as a method for estimating the reliability of a quantitative model. The bootstrap process begins with the original or training data set of observations and forms a bootstrap sample of the original data set by repeatedly selecting an observation from the original data set at random. Because the same observation can be selected more than once, this is called sampling with replacement.

A bootstrap sample usually contains as many observations as the original training data, so if you began with 1,000 observations, you would have 1,000 observations in the bootstrap sample. Many of the observations are duplicates. Bootstrapping consists of constructing many bootstrap samples, for example, 50 or 100. These samples are used to train a model for each sample to collect predictions and predictive errors across all samples. Collecting and displaying this pooled information will indicate how precise the model, which is built solely on the original data, will be.

Bootstrapping can also be used to assess the stability of various predictors. Bootstrapping forms 10 bootstrap samples, which are used to train decision trees for each of the samples. Stability and variability among predictors from model to model can serve as indicators of how well predictors will perform in the new data sets.

A bootstrap data set is created by randomly selecting observations from the training data set. Bootstrap estimation uses a selection process that repeatedly creates independently sampled data sets. These data sets are treated as independent estimates for the purpose of producing a predicted score or class outcome. Class outcomes are typically determined by a plurality vote.

In the simplest form of bootstrapping, instead of repeatedly analyzing subsets of data, you repeatedly analyze subsamples of data. Each subsample is a random sample with replacements from the full sample. Depending on what you want to do, 50 to 2,000 subsamples might be used. The usual process for creating a subsample is to pick an observation at random from the original data set and copy it to the subsample data set. This process is repeated multiple times. Each time, the subsample observation is returned to the original data set after the subsample has been created. The same observation can be copied many times, but more than likely, different observations will be copied.

Figure 5.6: Illustration of Consolidated Bagging and Bootstrapping Processes

Bagging

Bagging refers to the creation of a pooled estimate of the target. This estimate is based on a collection of models using the same algorithm in data sets sampled with replacements from a single training data set. Bagging stands for bootstrap aggregation and was invented by Leo Breiman (1996). He uses the voting method for classification, in which plurality determines the target outcome.

Bagging is illustrated in Figures 5.7 and 5.8. Successive samples from the original data set are taken and the decision tree is trained in this sample. Typically, a random sample with replacement is taken. The non-sample observations can be used as validation data. These are called OOB (Out of Bag) observations.

Figure 5.7: Illustration of a High-Level View of Bagging

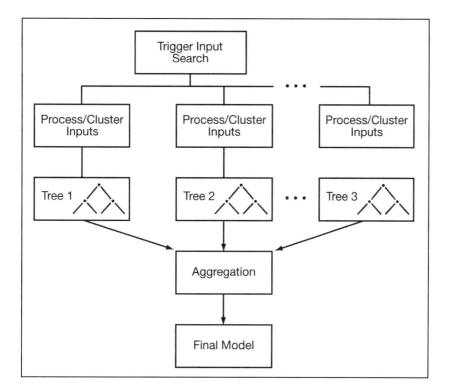

Bagging can improve the predictive accuracy of unstable models. Breiman showed that combining predictions from models based on bootstrapped samples improves the accuracy of the predictions if the models are unstable. He coined the term "bagging" to mean the process of bootstrap aggregation. For continuous targets, the predictions are averaged. For classification (categorical) targets, the predictions are based on voting. In voting, the predicted class is the one that most of the bootstrap samples predict. An alternative strategy is to average the probabilities of the various categories occurring in the bootstrap samples, and to base the predicted class on these averaged posterior probabilities.

Bagging not only helps with instability, it helps smooth out the prediction. Smoothing works especially well for a technique, such as decision trees, that dices data in a recursive, piecewise linear fashion (i.e., the decision boundaries in the data are formed by linear cut-points that are determined by the values on the left and right sides of the branch partitions). Thus, a decision tree with 20 leaves partitions the data space with 20 linear edges. These 20 linear edges partition the data space into 20 rectangles. The 20 rectangles are subsegmented by lower partitions in the decision trees that are grown in each of the descendents of the original 20 leaves. Bagging 100, 20-leaf decision trees will average 100-step functions across the data space. This process forms a more continuous set of boundaries in the data space and approximates the data-fitting characteristics of techniques, such as regression and neural networks.

In general, bagging smoothes and blurs the normal, hard-edged partitions that are formed by a single decision tree. If the true relationship between the inputs and the target is not well represented by a single, hard-edged partition, then smoothing will help reveal the relationship. One side effect of smoothing is obscuring the overall structure of the decision tree. Because the decision tree is averaged across many decision trees, the original, readily interpretable decision tree structure is lost.

In some cases, growing one decision tree with 2,000 leaves might smooth the partition to the same extent as averaging 100 decision trees with 20 leaves. Bagging might be preferred if the data does not support growing a large decision tree. An averaged prediction from several models, including models of different types, is generally a better prediction than the prediction of an individual model.

This is likely to happen if the models are very different. Imagine a plot in which the prediction from one model is measured on the horizontal axis, and the prediction from the other model is measured on the vertical axis. Each point represents the predictions of the two models for one observation. If the points are predominantly near the main diagonal, then averaging the predictions does not help. If the points form a blur, then averaging the predictions might help.

Figure 5.8: Illustration of Selecting Observations in Samples Used in Bagging

Observation	Sample 1	Sample 2	. . .	Sample N
1	★	—		★
2	★	★		—
3	—	★	■ ■ ■	—
4	★	—		★
5	—	★		★
6	★	★	■ ■ ■	—
7	—	—		★
8	★	★	■ ■ ■	
9	—	★		★
10	★	—	■ ■ ■	★
★ Typically 10, 25, 50 samples are drawn				

Boosting

When predictions from a set of models are combined into a single prediction, the result is often called an ensemble. One of the most important areas in the discussion of ensembles is boosting. The boosting approach was developed by Schapire (1989). Recent work of Freund and Schapire (1997) and Friedman (2001) extends the original development. Boosting has been incorporated in many approaches, including the recent development of the C4.5 and C5 toolkits by Quinlan. Boosting operates much like bagging; however, boosting uses varying probabilities in selecting an observation to be included in the sample.

In bagging, each observation is equally likely to be selected each time a new sample is created. Therefore, no matter how many rules are developed, each decision tree that is produced from a boosting iteration has no dependence on any previous decision tree.

The goal of boosting is to increase the probability of selecting an observation that performs well when predicting the target. The assessment of how well an observation predicts a target depends on comparing the predicted results of an observation with the actual results. In the initial boosted sample, all observations that had poor prediction performance, as indicated by a validation of the original decision tree, have a greater probability of being selected for the boosted sample. This has the effect of including more observations and generating more statistical power for examples in the training data set that do not perform well. The resulting ensemble has a combined decision rule with a higher accuracy.

Whereas bagging builds the decision trees in parallel and they vote on the prediction, boosting builds a series of decision trees and the prediction receives incremental improvement by each decision tree in the series. The method of reweighting works so that classifiers change depending on previous performance.

The original data is placed in training and test partitions (for example, in a 70% to 30% ratio) so that the decision tree is grown using the training data set and the accuracy of the decision tree growth is checked using the test data set. Decision tree growth terminates when test results begin to deviate from training results.

A series of many decision tree models is grown this way. Often, 25 decision trees are grown, but 50 or more could have been grown. After each iteration of decision tree growth, the correct and incorrect classifications are calculated for each record in the test data set. A classification is determined correct if the rules that predict a record do, in fact, agree with the code that is contained in the test data set.

All of the correct records are marked for that iteration and the total number of incorrect records is calculated. A proportion of incorrect records is calculated, and a reciprocal of this proportion is used to calculate a weight that is used to boost the relative percentage of records that were incorrect. Correct records are automatically down-weighted. The proportions of the weighted records are standardized so that the total number of records adds up to the original total number of records.

After the records are up-weighted or down-weighted, the reweighted records are run through another iteration of the decision tree. The same settings that were used on the initial decision tree growth iteration are used. However, the results will be different because the weights of the records that contribute to the results are different. Records that have a tendency to be misclassified have more instances in the data and more opportunity to build the necessary statistical power to produce a correct classification. At the end of each iteration, the total number of correct and incorrect classifications for each record is calculated, and the corresponding boosted weights and down-weights are calculated depending on the summed total of incorrect classifications that are calculated for each record.

After the iterations are done, a voting process calculates the most likely category of the predicted classification based on a summed average of the predicted classes that were calculated at the end of each iteration. The classification with the most number of votes is used. This is determined by the simple majority rule.

Boosting is a classification algorithm that has been shown to produce lower error rates than bagging. In data sets in which decision trees are effective for classification, boosting improves the classification rate slightly. Bagging works by taking a bootstrap sample from the training data set. Bagging produces good results, but only if a single decision tree is reasonably effective to start with.

Boosting has been shown to work in a wide variety of circumstances, even though it is not always clear why it works. The explanation of its success is different from bagging. Friedman et al. interpret boosting as maximizing the likelihood of a certain type of additive logistic model. This way of explaining the success of boosting is understandable and reassuring to statisticians. Several methods to select probabilities have been proposed. Breiman proposed the following simple formula:

Let *m(n)* equal the number of models that misclassify the nth observation.

$$Set\ P(n) = \frac{(1 + m(n)^4)}{\sum_{1}^{n} (1 + m(n)^4)}$$

P(n) is the probability of choosing the nth observation in the next bootstrap sample. Although this formula assumes a classification task, it is possible to include another measure of fit, such as squared error, so that continuous outcomes could be estimated.

AdaBoost

AdaBoost is a form of boosting that builds an initial model from the training data set. This first pass through the training data results in a standard model. From this model, some records will be correctly classified by the decision algorithm, and some records will be misclassified. The misclassified records are identified as a separate training data set, and the decision search criteria are adjusted by weighting the attributes of the misclassified records.

A new model is built with the misclassified records as a modified training data set. This boosts the importance of the misclassified records in the training process.

The building of the initial model, followed by boosting, is repeated until the incrementally generated model performs at the level of a random guess. This indicates that forming additional boosted samples is not likely to contribute worthwhile results. At this point, there is a panel of models. This panel is used to make a decision on new data by combining the expertise of each model so that the more accurate experts carry more weight. This process appears as follows:

Figure 5.9: Illustration of a Panel of Models Based on Reweighted Samples Used in Boosting

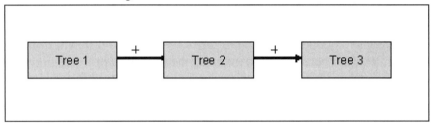

Because each successive model is weighted according to classification accuracy, this approach is sometimes called stochastic gradient boosting.

Multiple Random Classification Decision Trees

The paths of artificial intelligence, cognitive science, and data mining have been interwoven from the original development of the first decision trees. Their relationship has stayed in place and is stronger than it has ever been. No place is this more obvious than in the development of one of the most recent forms of multiple decision trees—random forests. The inspiration for random forests is in work originally reported in 1997 by Amit and Geman. The authors were interested in the effects of randomization on the construction of the decision tree and adopted the idea of choosing a random sample of predictors from the collection of inputs at each node of the decision tree. They referred to their work as the construction of a kind of "holographic" decision tree. The decision tree is holographic in the sense that each node has the possibility of reflecting a different facet of the predictive space that is contained in the training data. This was accomplished by taking a random sample of available predictors or inputs available at each node.

At each node, after the sample of predictors was taken, an estimate of the best predictor was made using a random sample of data points. After producing *n* decision trees—T1,

T2, …, T*n* —the authors picked a predictive structure designed to maximize the average terminal distribution in the resulting decision tree.

At this point, they chose a random sample of predictors from the entire candidate data set. From this sample, they developed an estimate of the optimal predictor using a random sample of data points. They then developed a maximum estimate based on the average (leaf) distribution. To test their approach, the authors used 223,000 binary images of isolated digits written by more than 2,000 writers. They used 100,000 images for training and 50,000 for testing.

What they found was that the best classification rate for a single decision tree was 5%, whereas the best classification rate of multiple decision trees was 91%. They convincingly showed that by aggregating decision trees, the success of automatic digit classification improves dramatically.

Random Forests

Amit and Geman's work served as inspiration for the random forests approach developed by Leo Breiman. Originally a statistician, Breiman was inspired by the research and development that he observed in the artificial intelligence and cognitive science world. As a statistician, he could say, "Statisticians want to know *why* things work; whereas, artificial intelligence researchers want to know *whether* things worked." In the case of random forests, he succeeded in developing something that certainly worked.

Like the precursor, a random forest is an average of decision trees. In each node, a branch search is performed on a random set of inputs, instead of on the full set of inputs. The training data is a random sample of the original data set. A portion of the random sample is set aside as a test sample. Like in bagging, decision trees are grown independently (in parallel). As Breiman pointed out, the randomness makes the variable selection less greedy (i.e., less likely to overfit), thus mitigating the need for pruning. Because many decision trees are grown, the expectation is that in the long run, the better variables are more likely to be selected.

Each decision tree in the random forest is grown in a bootstrap sample of the training data set. Because a subset of all the available inputs is selected for sampling, the number is smaller than the total number of inputs that are available across the entire data set. At each node of the developed decision tree, a subset of inputs is selected at random out of the total number of inputs that are available. The branch that is used is the one that produces the best split on this subset of inputs.

Each time a decision tree is grown, about one-third of the cases are left out of the sample used to grow the decision tree. This is called the OOB (Out of Bag) sample and is used to test and validate the decision tree that is grown with the bootstrap sample. Bag now refers to the data that forms the bootstrap aggregate. This OOB data set can be used to form estimates of the incremental error as new decision trees are added to the panel. The OOB data set can also be used to form estimates of variable importance.

To score a new data set, pass each row of the new data through each decision tree in the random forest and record the predicted value that is given by each decision tree. To aggregate the results, either compute an average of all the scores (for a continuous target) or determine the most likely class value through a majority rule from the classifications that are produced by the decision trees (for a categorical target).

Breiman's research with random forests showed that in many cases, random forests are more accurate than boosting approaches. He found that the random forest approach could handle hundreds and thousands of input variables with no degeneration in accuracy. In his latest work, he presented many unique ways to present the results of random forests and proposed methods for using random forests to do a form of cluster analysis (Breiman 2001).

The Integration of Decision Trees with Other Data Mining Approaches

6

Introduction

So far most of the discussion on decision trees has been in the area of their direct utility as descriptive and predictive tools. This chapter shows how decision trees can also be used to provide software support when integrating decision trees with other data mining techniques. The following topics are addressed in this chapter:

- Stratified regression
- Decision trees in forecasting applications
- Decision trees in variable selection, interaction detection
- Decision trees in Analytical model development

Recall that the original use of decision trees was as a complement or alternative to regression. As decision trees have developed, their abilities as a complement to, as well as a substitute for, other data mining techniques have increased.

Decision Trees in Stratified Regression

Stratified regression is one of the oldest applications of decision trees. As illustrated in Figure 1.3 in Chapter 1, the goal of stratified regression is to divide the main data set into subgroups so that different regression equations fit into each of the subgroups. This is especially appropriate when the differences in the subgroups are so profound that it is simpler and more effective to determine the specialized shape of the regression equation in each of the subgroups.

A formal definition and extensive explanation of stratified regression is provided in Neville's article on stratified regression (1999). Boston housing data is used as a basis for the examples in this article and the StatLib repository (http://lib.stat.cmu.edu/) is the source of the original data. The following display lists the variables that are included in the data set. The dependent variable is **Lmv**.

```
Name        Description

Crim        Per capita crime rate by town
Zn          Proportion of a town's residential land zoned for lots greater
            than 25,000 square feet
Indus       Proportion of non-retail business acres per town
Chas        Charles River dummy variable
Noxsq       Nitrogen oxide concentration (parts per hundred million)
            squared
RmSq        Average number of rooms squared
Age         Proportion of owner-occupied units built prior to 1940
Dis         Logarithm of the weighted distances to five unemployment
            centers in the Boston region
Rad         Logarithm of index of accessibility to radial highways
Tax         Full-value property tax rate
Ptratio     Pupil-teacher ratio by town
B           (Bk-0.63) squared, where Bk is the proportion of blacks
Lstat       Logarithm of the proportion of the population that is lower
            status
Lmv         Logarithm of the median value of owner-occupied homes
```

Neville's article explains that there are several ways to form strata based on decision trees. From this strata, regression models were produced that were better than regression models based on fitting the entire data set as one block of data. Figure 6.1 illustrates the decision tree branch with one of the possible strata that could be used to improve the regression results. The branch split on nitrogen oxide concentration (parts per hundred million) squared (**Noxsq**).

Figure 6.1: Illustration of Decision Tree Identifying Strata

Tax and ? (missing) are also strata that could improve the regression results.

To implement stratified regression, it is necessary to partition the data. Alternatively, you could create an effect variable that will partition the data numerically. In the case of strata formed by nitrogen oxide, you should form two regression equations. One regression equation will fit the data on the left (217 observations) and one regression equation will fit the data on the right (235 observations).

Time-Ordered Data

Traditionally, decision trees have been used to analyze cross-sectional data such as survey data. A cross-sectional data set contains measurements of a variety of observations at a given point in time, as shown in Figure 6.2.

Figure 6.2: Illustration of the Form of Data Captured from One Point in Time

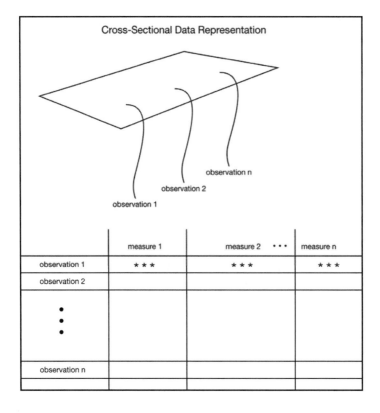

By contrast, time series data contains measurements of a variety of observations at various time intervals (e.g., stock prices), as shown in Figure 6.3.

Figure 6.3: Illustration of the Form of Data Captured from a Time Series

Decision Trees in Forecasting Applications

As analysts have gained more experience with time-ordered data, they have discovered that techniques that are commonly used to analyze cross-sectional data can be adapted to analyze time series data. Thus, regression techniques are used in the analysis of both cross-sectional and time series data. Similarly, decision trees can be used to analyze both cross-sectional and time series data.

Figure 6.4 illustrates a typical time series in cross-sectional form, where **m** stands for measure and **t** stands for time.

Figure 6.4: Illustration of Reworking Time Series Data into Cross-Sectional Form

	$M_1T_1 \ M_2T_1 \dots M_nT_1$	$M_1T_2 \ M_2T_2 \dots M_nT_2$	$\bullet \ \bullet \ \bullet$	$M_nT_1 \ M_nT_2 \dots M_nT_n$
observation 1				
observation 2				
$\bullet$ $\bullet$ $\bullet$				
observation n				

Next, in Figure 6.5, a time series shows the rise and fall of lynx traps in any given year as the lynx population rises and falls according to the operation of other factors in ecology, such as food supply, disease, and predators. The lynx population hits a peak in the years of 1828, 1866, and 1904.

Figure 6.5: Illustration of a Time Series

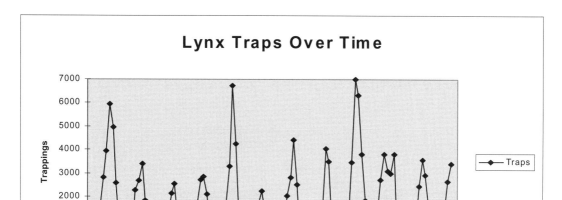

A portion of the data underlying these results is shown in the following display.

Year	Traps
1821	269
1822	321
1823	585
1824	871
1825	1475
1826	2821
1827	3928
1918	81
1919	80
1920	108
1921	229
1922	399
1923	1132
1924	2432
1925	3574
1926	2935
1927	1537
1928	529
1929	485

Figure 6.6 shows a decision tree that reproduces the results of the graph in Figure 6.5. The peaks in the graph are captured in the intervals of 1827–1830, 1864–1867, and 1903–1906 (the lowest interval of <= 1826 and the highest interval of >= 1907 are not shown in the decision tree).

Figure 6.6: Illustration of a Decision Tree of the Lynx Time Series Data

In many situations, a decision tree will handle time series data in a straightforward way. This is shown in the classic study of lynx traps. In many applied situations, some reworking of the data may be necessary. For example, in direct marketing, there is a need to derive customer measures for recency, frequency, and monetary value. These measures come from transaction data based on purchase interactions. For recency, you can sum all transactions and create measures, such as last purchase date. For frequency, you can count the number of monthly purchases. You can use total or average purchases for monetary value.

Banks like to distinguish card account holders by their purchase habits. Do the card holders use the card a lot, and pay down the outstanding balance on a monthly basis? Do they consistently maintain an outstanding balance? Has a customer moved from one mode of payment to another? If so, why? Distinguishing card account holders in these ways means that fields must be created to measure these characteristics on a monthly basis. Furthermore, the characteristics need to be stored on a month-to-month basis and, if a characteristic changes, an indicator needs to be set. This results in the creation of a new field of data.

Decision Trees in Variable Selection

In the following banking data set, the goal is to determine the attributes of online transactions.

Name	Role	Report	Level	.	.	L	U	.	Label
DDA	Input	No	Binary	No.	.		N		Checking Account
DDABAL	Input	No	Interval	No.	.		N		Checking Balance
DEP	Input	No	Nominal	No.	.		N		Checking Deposits
DEPAMT	Input	No	Interval	No.	.		N		Amount Deposited
DIRDEP	Input	No	Binary	No.	.		N		Direct Deposit
HMOWN	Input	No	Binary	No.	.		N		Owns Home
HMVAL	Input	No	Interval	No.	.		N		Home Value
ILS	Input	No	Binary	No.	.		N		Installment Loan
ILSBAL	Input	No	Interval	No.	.		N		Loan Balance
INAREA	Input	No	Binary	No.	.		N		Local Address
INCOME	Input	No	Interval	No.	.		N		Income
INV	Input	No	Binary	No.	.		N		Investment
INVBAL	Input	No	Interval	No.	.		N		Investment Balance
IRA	Input	No	Binary	No.	.		N		Retirement Account
IRABAL	Input	No	Interval	No.	.		N		IRA Balance
LOC	Input	No	Binary	No.	.		N		Line of Credit
LOCBAL	Input	No	Interval	No.	.		N		Line of Credit Balance
LORES	Input	No	Interval	No.	.		N		Length of Residence
MM	Input	No	Binary	No.	.		N		Money Market
MMBAL	Input	No	Interval	No.	.		N		Money Market Balance
MMCRED	Input	No	Nominal	No.	.		N		Money Market Credits
MOVED	Input	No	Binary	No.	.		N		Recent Address Change
MTG	Input	No	Binary	No.	.		N		Mortgage
MTGBAL	Input	No	Interval	No.	.		N		Mortgage Balance
NCI	Input	No	Binary	No.	.		N		Number Insufficient Fund
NSFAMT	Input	No	Interval	No.	.		N		Amount NSF
PHONE	Input	No	Nominal	No.	.		N		Number Telephone Banking
POS	Input	No	Interval	No.	.		N		Number Point of Sale
POSAMT	Input	No	Interval	No.	.		N		Amount Point of Sale
RES	Input	No	Nominal	No.	.		C		Area Classification
SAV	Input	No	Binary	No.	.		N		Saving Account
SAVBAL	Input	No	Interval	No.	.		N		Saving Balance
SDB	Input	No	Binary	No.	.		N		Safety Deposit Box
TELLER	Rejected	No	Interval	No.	.		N		Teller Visits
online	Target	No	Interval	No.	.		N		number of online transactions

A traditional variable-importance approach looks at the zero-order correlations between all possible inputs and the target. This approach produces the following chart:

Input	Correlation
DEPAMT	0.35970
POSAMT	0.21106
POS	0.18395
ACCTAGE	0.13256
DDABAL	0.11238
ATMAMT	0.10031
NSFAMT	0.08569
ILSBAL	0.08247
LOCBAL	0.07963
HMVAL	0.06979
AGE	0.02890
CCBAL	0.02787
MTGBAL	0.01641
INCOME	0.01173
CRSCORE	0.01077
LORES	0.00613
SAVBAL	0.00116
IRABAL	-0.01121
INVBAL	-0.02104
MMBAL	-0.03722
CDBAL	-0.07074

The strength of the correlation is shown in Figure 6.7.

Figure 6.7: Correlation between Inputs and Target

Decision Tree Results

The decision tree results tell a different story. In the decision tree, variable importance is calculated as the sum of the worth statistics for an input across all the split nodes of the decision tree. If an input is an important splitting criterion in many levels of the decision tree, then its importance grows as a result. Inputs that do not appear in any splits have zero importance.

DEPAMT	Amount Deposited	1.0
DEP	Checking Deposits	0.34
CCBAL	Credit Card Balance	0.19
ACCTAGE	Age of Oldest Account	0.18
DDABAL	Checking Balance	0.09
ATMAMT	ATM Withdrawal Amount	0.09
LOC	Line of Credit	0.06
POSAMT	Amount Point of Sale	0.05
MTG	Mortgage	0.05
DIRDEP	Direct Deposit	0.05
AGE	Age	0.05
PHONE	Number Telephone Banking	0.05
ATM	ATM	0.04

Because the decision tree method of calculating variable importance incorporates the effect of an input across various splits, it captures the effect of an input in various regions and subregions of the data set. This captures a different dimension of variable importance from a simple zero-order correlation between an input and a target. Similarly, it captures a different dimension from multiple regression. In this case, the value of the coefficient of an input in the regression equation is constrained by the values of all the other inputs in one global equation.

Interactions

The next decision tree shows an analysis of a data set on home equity loan histories and whether the loans have defaulted or not. A default is indicated by a Bad=0 field in the analysis. The high overall default rate of 80% is used to illustrate interactions.

Figure 6.8: Illustration of a Decision Tree Identifying an Interaction (Account Age and Mortgage Due)

Defaults increase in parallel with how old the outstanding credit line is. The decision tree shows 73% default for credit lines that are up to 172 days old, and 87% default for credit lines that are older than 172 days.

The lower level of the decision tree shows an interaction between credit line age and the amount of mortgage due. When the age is less than 172 days, the greater amount of mortgage due increases the default rate by 10%—from 67% to 77%. When the age is equal to or more than 172 days, the greater amount of mortgage due increases the default rate from 61% to 87%—a difference of 26%. This is more than twice the increase in the younger credit lines.

This suggests that it could be useful to construct an interaction term that combines age and mortgage due (clage*mortdue) when building the regression model to predict default. In this example, the direction of the interaction on the left and right of the decision tree is the same. On the lowest level of the decision tree on both sides, the decision tree is formed by the same branch (created by using **MORTDUE** as a branch split input). This decision tree and its interactions can be considered symmetrical.

It is possible to have asymmetric interactions in decision trees. The subtree formed by **MORTDUE** might produce different directions of the interaction depending on the side of the decision tree. This is a reversal; envision that the left side of the decision tree contained leaves with 77% and 67% defaults, rather than 67% and 77% as seen in Figure 6.1).

Another form of asymmetry is when there is a different partitioning field on the right side of the decision tree, compared to what is on the left side.

Cross-Contributions of Decision Trees and Other Approaches

The following table describes the various impacts between the data mining methods:

Table 6.1: Data Mining Methods Cross-Impact Matrix

Data Mining Methods Cross Impact Matrix					
	Association	Clustering	Regression	Decision Trees	Neural Networks
Association				Create associations and sequences as composite inputs to decision trees to determine relationships	
Clustering				Might be useful in creating composite clusters for inclusion in decision trees	
Regression				Use regression techniques to create linear composites for inclusion as inputs - a data reduction technique	

(*continued*)

Data Mining Methods Cross Impact Matrix					
	Association	Clustering	Regression	Decision Trees	Neural Networks
Decision Trees			Define strata for regression treatment Compute dummy variables Qualify variables in the equation (e.g., identify interactions) Impute missing values based on inputs with various levels of measurement		Prequalify variables for inclusion, including bins for categories Turn decision tree on predicted scores (and residuals) to assist in interpretation Turn decision tree on score residuals
Neural Networks				Fit and fine-tune unclassified observations	

Decision Trees in Analytical Model Development

The following example shows how a decision tree is used in a business-to-business marketing application. The analysis deals with network equipment sales. The display shows current sales in the target geography:

	Enterprises	Sites	Accounts	Penetration	Accounts	Penetration	Sites
State Enterprise Footprint (with site counts) and Site Counts for Information (not included in Penetration Calculations)					Enterprise Penetration Rates		
Segments							
Enterprise 10k+	**255**	174462	640	251%	**188**	**74%**	5125
Gen. Business (<250)	**277828**	410404	880	0%	**6257**	**2%**	7276
Majors	**10086**	178168	2450	24%	**3058**	**30%**	7319
Majors < 500	5119	35727			1063	21%	
Majors 500<1000	2571	32193			824	32%	
Majors 1000<2500	1521	39710			680	45%	
Majors 2500<5000	594	35165			330	56%	
Majors < 10000	281	35373			161	57%	
Sml Business (< 10)	**1844573**	1865348	1191000	65%	**2511**	**0%**	2531
Totals	2132742	2628382			12014		22251
Verticals							
Education	**16895**	38774			**1138**	**7%**	2274
Ed Services	8030	10360			114	1%	
Elem and Sec Sc	6278	22677			642	10%	
Jr. Colleges, D	877	1400			150	17%	
Univ. + 4yr col	830	2995			215	26%	
Vocatn	880	1342			17	2%	
Financial Services	**76237**	126989			**911**	**1%**	1956
Banking	9268	31808			267	3%	
Credit Unions	1640	2916			168	10%	
Insurance	40048	53593			278	1%	
Other, CC, Mortgage	20994	30044			151	1%	
Securities	4287	8628			47	1%	
Government	**13285**	46716			**664**	**5%**	1750
Local/Municipal	1048	1697			28	3%	
National, Federal	468	8659			21	4%	
Public sector	11546	36082			611	5%	
Super national	223	278			4	2%	
Health	**120255**	142684			**999**	**1%**	1471
Payer	264	609			20	8%	
Provider	119991	142075			979	1%	
Horizontal	**1906070**	2273219			**8302**	**0%**	14800
Totals	2132742	2628382			12014		22251

This display shows penetration rates based on current sales in a target U.S. sales region. Vendor sales data has been enriched by linking with Dun & Bradstreet data to show how sales are distributed according to enterprise size and vertical market

Penetration rates in large enterprises (over 10,000 employees) are good—74%. However, penetration rates in smaller enterprises (e.g., 500–1,000 employees) are lower —only 32%.

Vertical market figures show that the best penetration is in large universities (26%); government, financial services, and health penetration rates taper off to less than 10%.

There are some important lessons here:

- Further penetration is only likely with lower-cost, lower-margin offers.
- Penetration into smaller enterprises in new vertical markets depends on indirect sales methods and leveraging partner relationships in these accounts.

It might be useful to look at distribution of sales according to cities in a region and city size (i.e., broken up into **Tier 1** and **Tier 2**). As with enterprise size and vertical market, you can identify cities and proposed technologies where penetration rates could be higher, as shown in the following display.

msaCode	Total_sales	Total_sites	Total_IPTel	Total_IPTel_Sites	Total_ETech	Total_ETech_sites
Tier 1						
City1	$370,157,557	2709	$17,593,345	119	$34,959,638	875
City2	$40,131,744	400	$4,962,181	29	$3,765,035	136
	$177,993,038	877	$1,238,919	41	$17,022,461	313
	$39,240,999	733	$450,877	37	$2,760,661	217
	$41,322,519	609	$2,558,176	50	$4,279,462	212
	$67,238,224	1180	$3,933,702	83	$8,479,067	363
City n	$51,256,149	776	$439,132	27	$5,357,579	207
	$22,939,263	529	$1,447,242	26	$3,326,135	158
	$72,864,922	861	$3,176,715	59	$9,089,244	382
Totals	$883,744,414	8614	$35,800,249	471	$89,039,282	2863
Tier 2						
City1	$20,006,509	302	$280,667	9	$4,004,468	106
City2	$5,425,069	99	$1,297,967	12	$513,774	36
	$31,393,339	575	$1,752,518	29	$5,241,849	199
	$30,161,775	420	$690,829	21	$2,982,812	148
	$22,791,552	296	$406,826	10	$5,355,255	72
	$24,650,791	497	$376,163	18	$3,007,766	184
	$63,161,200	482	$336,603	31	$4,845,130	166
City n	$63,440,754	750	$1,216,406	40	$12,418,860	244
Totals	$261,030,988	3421	$6,356,978	170	$38,369,915	1155
All Others						
Totals	$700,799,636	10216	$16,026,621	449	$161,159,600	3239
Grand Total	$1,845,575,099	22251	$58,183,888	1090	$288,568,797	7257

The power of analytics comes from using known sales data to build a model that is applied against the universe of enterprises. Sales data comes from the vendor's sales data store. Universe data comes from third-party data vendors (in this case, Dun & Bradstreet; however, Harte-Hanks and infoUSA also provide business-to-business data).

With known sales data (and the attributes of these sales), you can match the sales and their attributes with the attributes of the universe data to determine where the opportunities are (and how strong and what kind they are). To do this, you need a predictive model.

You should begin by using decision trees to look through the data. From the Dun & Bradstreet data, you can get information on potential key predictors of sales. This is basically corporate demographics, sometimes called firmographics. Decision trees are one of many prediction methods available in SAS Enterprise Miner. They are very useful in the early stages of forming predictive models because they provide a robust view into the relationships in the data.

Figure 6.9: Illustration of Decision Trees Predicting New Technology (Business-to-Business)

Figure 6.9 shows the relationship between the enterprise size and the probability to purchase new technology. There is a strong positive relationship that shows that among small enterprises, new technology purchases are in the range of 30% of all enterprises. Among larger enterprises (e.g., those with more than 7,750 employees), 60% have new technology purchases. Marketing and sales planners can take advantage of this knowledge when planning sales campaigns.

Predictive models can also take advantage of this knowledge and combine it with knowledge of other known relationships to form a multiple predictor model.

In this example, numerous decision trees were run to determine what strong relationships existed in the data. The following analytics-derived sales predictors were identified in the analysis:

- head count
- corporate location
- regional concentration
- business type
- PC estimator
- multi-site indicator (business knowledge)

After a good knowledge of the data is extracted using decision trees, it is useful to combine decision trees with other predictive approaches, specifically regression and neural networks. Combined predictive models, sometimes called ensembles, can produce better predictions. A combined approach is illustrated in Figure 6.10.

Figure 6.10: Illustration of the Combined Predictive Model to Compute Business-to-Business Propensity Scores

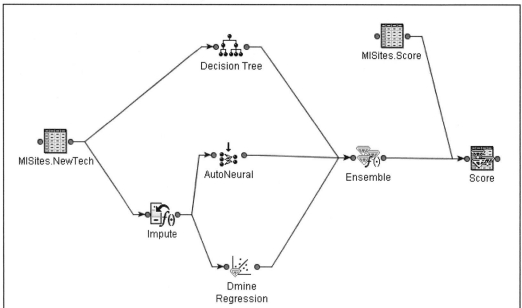

The final results of this model are shown in Figure 6.11. In this business-to-business example, there is a total of 15,309 customers in the data set. The predicted sales, based on an analysis of the current sales data as applied to all candidate businesses in the proposed sales area, are classed into high, medium, and low probability (depending on the strength of the combined predictive score). As shown in Figure 6.11, there were over 76,000 high probability purchasers in this sales area. As illustrated earlier in Figure 6.9, general businesses (fewer than 250 employees) have the largest number of high probability sales (38,348).

These results show how decision trees can be used to explore the data before constructing predictive models, which might combine multiple predictive approaches. They also show the value of predictive modeling in general; for example, in this sales area, there were only about 15,000 customers, yet the predictive model indicated that there were as many as 76,000 high probability purchasers. These results can be used to construct sales campaigns to contact these highly probable customers.

Figure 6.11: Results of Business-to-Business Example

	Enterprises	Sites	Accounts	Penetration	Enterprise High Probability Purchase
Segments					
Enterprises 10K	255	174462	186	73%	4332
General Business (<250)	277928	410404	6261	2%	38348
Majors	10096	179160	3058	30%	33625
Majors < 500	5119	36721	1063	21%	
Majors 500 - 1000	2571	32199	824	32%	
Majors 1000 < 2500	1521	39710	680	45%	
Majors 2500 < 5001	594	35185	330	56%	
Majors < 1000	281	35373	161	57%	
Small Business (< 10)	1844573	1865346	2511	0%	38
Total	2142938	2808560	15074		76343
Vertical					
Education	16995	39774	1130	7%	4777
Educational Services	8630	10360	114	1%	
Elementary And Secondary Schools	8278	22677	642	8%	
Jr. Colleges	877	1400	150	17%	
Universities + 4 Year Colleges	830	2995	215	26%	
Vocational	886	1342	17	2%	
Financial Services	76237	125989	911	1%	7002
Banking	9268	31808	267	3%	
Credit Unions	1640	2916	16	1%	
Insurance	40648	53583	27	0%	
Other, Cc, Mortgage	20994	30044	151	1%	
Securities	4297	9629	47	1%	
Government	13285	46716	664	5%	4468
Local Municipal	1048	1697	28	3%	
National, Federal	106	8659	21	20%	
Public Sector	11546	30082	611	5%	
Super National	223	278	4	2%	
Health	120255	142694	003	1%	4700
Payor	264	609	20	8%	
Provider	119991	142075	979	1%	
Horizontal	1906070	2273219	8302	0%	55388
Total	2362368	2978534	15309	1%	76343

Conclusion

Two of the many themes explored in this book relate to the synergy and complementarities found between decision trees and Business Intelligence, and the synergy and complementarities between decision trees and data mining tools and predictive modeling techniques. Is seems likely that the complementarities will continue in these respective areas and, in so doing, is likely to lead to increased synergy and integration in the future. Further developments in these areas include the following:

Business Intelligence

Decision tree drill down through any face of any cube constructed through the multidimensional data interface.

> Drill down provides the ability to retrieve the underlying detail data that the cube surface summaries are based on. Drill down allows the analyst to examine data in any of the multidimensional segments formed by the cube. It enables the analyst to reveal predictive and classification structure on this detail data through decision tree execution against the detail data.

Dimensional aggregation in-line with decision tree methods.

> It should be possible to express any dimensional view in an aggregated way using decision tree algorithms to collapse across dimensions with one or more of the measures being displayed. This provides a level of data summarization and data effect identification in what is otherwise a manual operation done "by eyeball."

Decision trees in cube form for subsequent display, viewing, and analysis.

> Just as data cubes can be pre-stored or pre-computed structures, so should decision trees. This ability is available in some applications. For example, decision tree results are used to determine the importance of various faces of the cubes. Decision tree results and input value clusters that are determined by decision tree methods can be used to produce collapsed values for dimensional cube faces.

Data Mining

The use of multiple decision tree approaches.

Multiple decision tree approaches that use a variety of boosting and bagging techniques are emerging. These approaches will be more routine in the future, especially as computational power increases to support this kind of decision tree growth in real time. Decision trees grown this way retain ease of use and the presentation characteristics that they share with business intelligence methods, while more closely resembling the other classic data mining methods, such as regression, neural networks, and cluster analysis.

More information about inputs.

With the growth of metadata repositories and metadata definitions, data sets are acquiring more information that defines the characteristics of inputs. For example, in addition to characteristics such as data type (integer, character, or numeric), you might expect to see the data element origin (such as customer table or transaction table). This could make it possible to associate a theoretical role and method to fields of data. Many applications use custom-defined fields to guide the construction of business intelligence dimensional reports. Likewise, extended metadata can be used to introduce business rules in the construction of decision trees. This has a number of benefits, for example, decreased computation and automated construction of reports and decision structures that are relevant to specific business uses.

Glossary

adjusted significance

a significance measure that has been adjusted for the number of tests that were carried out in order to determine the level of significance. This adjustment prevents the identification of statistically significant results by chance.

algorithm

a sequence of actions that performs a task. A procedure for solving a recurrent mathematical problem.

analytical model

a structure and process for analyzing a data set. For example, a decision tree is a model for the classification of a data set.

anomalous data

data that result from errors (for example, data entry errors) or that represent unusual events. Anomalous data should be examined carefully because it may carry important information.

ANOVA

ANalysis Of Variance. A procedure used to detect statistically significant effects induced by an independent variable on a continuous dependent variable. The ANOVA procedure employs an F-test to measure the differences between a given set of population means, where F = Mean Square for Treatments divided by the Mean Square for Error (F = MST/MSE). See F-ratio statistic.

artificial neural network

non-linear predictive models that learn through training and resemble biological neural networks in structure.

ASCII

American Standard Code for Information Interchange. The American National Standards Institute established a standard set of character codes that enable you to transmit text between computers or between a computer and a peripheral device.

assessment plot | a line graph that shows a plot of the accuracy of the decision tree for various subtrees.

bagging | a method that resamples the training data to create a pooled estimate of the target. Various decision trees are grown independently and a group vote is used to produce the target estimate. Bagging stands for bootstrap aggregation and was developed by Leo Breiman.

binary variable | a variable that takes only two distinct values. A binary variable is the most basic form of measurement indicating the presence or absence of some characteristic.

Bonferonni adjustment | a conservative adjustment that is applied to a test of significance to compensate for the number of statistical or mathematical operations that are performed in advance of a specific statistical test. These adjustments are designed to ensure that the test statistic conforms to the assumptions necessary for its calculation (for example, no dependencies between one test and another).

boosting | boosting resamples the data to form a succession of decision trees many times to form one average estimate for the target. Each time the data is used to grow a tree and the accuracy of the tree is computed. The successive samples are adjusted to accommodate previously computed inaccuracies. Because each successive sample is weighted according to the classification accuracy of previous models, this approach is sometimes called stochastic gradient boosting.

case | a collection of measurements regarding one of numerous entities represented in a data set. Synonyms: observation, record, example, pattern, sample, instance, row, vector, pair, tuple, fact.

case weight
: a positive numeric variable that serves as a multiplier to magnify the contribution of each line of data to an analysis. There are three kinds of case weights: frequencies, sampling weights, and variance weights.

categorical field/variable
: a variable that can assume only a limited number of discrete values. One example of a categorical variable is shoe size; another is hair color. A variable that lies in a nominal measurement space is sometimes called a qualitative, discrete, non-metric, or classification variable.

category
: one of the possible values of a categorical variable. Synonyms: class, label.

CHAID
: Chi-square Automatic Interaction Detection. A method of segmenting a file applied to a discrete response variable.

Chi-Squared Test
: a test measuring the statistical association between two categorical variables.

class variable
: in such fields as data mining, pattern recognition, and knowledge discovery, a class variable means a categorical target variable, and classification means assigning cases to categories of a target variable. In traditional research methodology, class variables are categorical variables and may be used as either an input or a target.

classification
: the process of dividing a data set into mutually exclusive groups such that the members of each group are as close as possible to one another, and different groups are as far as possible from one another, where distance is measured with respect to the specific variables you are trying to classify. For example, a typical classification problem is to divide a database of companies into groups that are as homogeneous as possible with respect to creditworthiness.

classification model	a model to predict the class value of a categorical—or class—target. See class variable and predictive model.
clustering	the process of dividing a data set into mutually exclusive groups such that the members of each group are as close as possible to one another, and different groups are as far as possible from one another, where distance is measured with respect to all available variables.
column	a column contains a field of information where each new column entry corresponds to a new row of data. In database terms, there may be many columns of data, each containing many rows of figures. Row and column data attributes are familiar as database terminology and are sometimes referred to as cases and variables in research data settings.
contingency table analysis	tabular analysis, which is the analysis of crosstabulations.
continuous field	a field that has a numeric or ordered range of values, such as temperature readings, e.g., 25, 26, 27, ...
correlation	a statistical measure or the association (or co-relation) between two fields of data.
CRT	Classification and Regression Trees. A decision tree technique developed by Brieman, Friedman, Olshen and Stone (1984) used for classification of a data set. It employs a grow-and-prune strategy to develop a right-sized tree and associated set of rules. Branches are formed by creating two-way splits.
database	information that you have gathered that is closely related. Most databases consist of fields, which contain units of information, and records, which contain sets or collections of fields. In general, fields are stored in columns and records are stored in rows.
data cleansing	the process of ensuring that all values in a data set are consistent and correctly recorded.

data mining	the extraction of hidden predictive information, typically from large databases that are often assembled from disparate sources.
data navigation	the process of viewing different dimensions, slices, and levels of detail of a multidimensional database. See dimensional cube.
data visualization	the visual interpretation of complex relationships in multidimensional data through scatter plots, dimensional cubes, and contour plots, for example.
data warehouse	a system for storing and delivering numerous sources of data into a unified and accessible location.
decision tree	a tree-shaped structure that represents a set of decisions. These decisions generate rules for the classification of a data set. See CRT and CHAID.
dependent variable	the field that you want to analyze as a function of other fields or variables in a data set. Also called the target field.
dimension	in a flat or relational database, each field in a record represents a dimension. In a multidimensional database, a dimension is a set of similar entities; for example, a multidimensional sales database might include the dimensions product, time, and city.
dimensional cube	an interactive analytical processing technique that originally referred to database applications that enable users to view, navigate, manipulate, and analyze databases as multidimensional entities. The approach has been incorporated into SQL in producing multidimensional summaries, and is now used for a variety of multidimensional reports and data manipulations based on dimensional cubes.
example	a member of a training set with measures for various attributes used to derive a decision tree structure. Equivalent to a subject, record or observation.

exhaustive partitioning	an alternative to standard CHAID branch grouping methods that is more likely to find the partitioning with the highest level of significance (since more groupings of values with respect to the dependent variable are formed). But the partitions formed are empirically stronger than heuristically derived partitions. Decision trees formed using the exhaustive partitioning method tend to have more branches than those formed using the original method. Developed by Biggs, et al.
exploratory data analysis	the use of graphical and descriptive statistical techniques to learn about the structure of a data set, normally as a preliminary step to predictive modeling.
extrapolation	scoring or generalization for values of observations outside or beyond a given training data set, typically on the basis of values or functions taken from other inputs in the training data set. Often used for predicting likely values for new observations.
field	a column that you label in your database that contains the same kind of information for each record.
floating	a branch clustering option originally developed by Kass that allows the missing values of an ordered field to group with other values in the field that they most closely resemble; i.e., they have a similar effect on the dependent variable as the ones they are grouped with.
F-ratio statistic	a value calculated as part of the ANOVA procedure. The larger this number is, the greater the distance between the means or average values of the nodes in the split. See ANOVA.
generalization	the ability of a model to compute good outputs from input data not used during training. Synonyms: interpolation and extrapolation, prediction.
genetic algorithm	an optimization technique that uses processes such as genetic combination, mutation, and natural selection in a design based on the concepts of natural evolution.

heuristic partitioning	a method of partitioning field data that provides optimal branching based on heuristics or statistical rules of thumb. It is less time consuming than exhaustive partitioning and tends to produce fewer branches and more compact trees than the exhaustive approach.
ID3	a machine learning algorithm.
independent variable	one of potentially many fields or variables that are used to describe, predict, or explain variability in a dependent or target field. Usually called inputs in a data mining context since the input value will influence the outcome of the model describing the relationship between the input and target.
induction	a method of proving statements about an ordered data set. It is reasoning from particulars to generals or the individual to the universal. Synonym: inference.
input	a variable used to predict/guess the value of the target variables. Synonyms: independent variable, predictor, regressor, explanatory variable, carrier, factor, covariate.
interaction effect	an effect on the relationships between two (or more) variables where the direction of the relationship (i.e. positive or negative) depends on the value of another variable. An example of interaction effect would be the relationship between weight and blood pressure changes for different age groups.
interpolation	the scoring or generalization for values of observations in a given training data set typically on the basis of values or functions taken from other inputs in the training data set. Often used for estimating missing values.
interval	a defined range of values.
interval boundary	a breaking point in a continuous field that divides the field into intervals.

interval variable	a numeric variable for which arithmetic operations with values are informative. An interval level of measurement means that the observed levels are ordered and numeric and that any interval of one unit on the scale of measurement represents the same amount, regardless of its location on the scale. Typical interval scales include income and temperature.
leaf	the bottom or final nodes in a decision tree.
linear model	an analytical model that assumes linear relationships in the coefficients of the variables being studied.
linear regression	a statistical technique used to find the best-fitting linear relationship between a target (dependent) variable and its predictors (independent variables).
–log (p)	see logworth.
logistic regression	a linear regression that predicts the proportions of a binary category target variable, such as type of customer, or has attribute vs. does not have attribute.
logworth	a transformation of the normal method of presenting significance that takes a negative log of the significance in order to express greater levels of significance in larger numbers (so the magnitude of the significance is reflected in the magnitude of the number).
measurement	the process of assigning numbers to objects such that the properties of the numbers reflect some attribute of the objects.
measurement level	one of several different ways in which properties of numbers can reflect attributes of objects. The most common measurement levels are nominal, ordinal, interval, log-interval, ratio, and absolute. For details, see the measurement theory FAQ at ftp://ftp.sas.com/pub/neural/measurement.html.
metric	supports arithmetic operations. See interval.

missing value	a value that is absent from a field. Missing values are represented as the "." character in SAS.
model	a general term that describes a conceptual representation of some phenomenon typically consisting of symbolic terms, factors, or constructs that may be rendered in language, pictures, or mathematics. Models include formulas or algorithms for computing outputs from inputs. A statistical model also includes information about the conditional distribution of the targets given the inputs. See trained model.
multidimensional database	a database designed for online analytical processing (dimensional cube). Structured as a multidimensional hypercube with one axis per dimension.
multiprocessor computer	a computer that includes multiple processors connected by a network. See parallel processing.
nearest neighbor	a technique that classifies each record in a data set based on a combination of the classes of the k records most similar to it in a historical data set (where k is greater than or equal to 1). Synonym: k-nearest neighbor.
node	a location defined by branch attributes on a tree. The root node is the initial node displayed in a decision tree. All branches originate at the root node. The nodes on the bottom-most branches of the tree are terminal nodes or leaves.
noise	an unpredictable variation, usually in a target variable. For example, if two cases have identical input values but different target values, the variation in those different target values is not predictable from any model using only those inputs; hence, that variation is noise. Noise is often assumed to be random, in which case it is inherently unpredictable. Whereas noise prevents target values from being accurately predicted, the distribution of the noise can be estimated statistically given enough data.

nominal variable | a numeric or character categorical variable in which the categories are unordered, and the category values convey no additional information beyond category membership.

nonlinear model | an analytical model that does not assume linear relationships in the coefficients of the variables being studied.

null category | a category that has no corresponding observation in a field displayed in a descendent node of the decision tree.

observation | a data record or subject of a given collection of data where one or more attribute measures are taken and recorded for each unit of analysis.

operational data | a type of data to be scored in a practical application, containing inputs but not target values. Scoring operational data is the main purpose of training models in data mining. Synonym: scoring data.

operationalize | describes the process of assigning representations, such as numeric tokens or concise term relations for conceptual entities.

ordered | a clustering option to collapse input values that treats a set of values as an ordered sequence, and that only allows adjacent values to be grouped together.

ordinal | a description of a method of measurement whereby adjacent values are ordered. Typically, the ordering is monotonic such that each higher level adjacent category is at least as great as the lower category and may be greater by some measurement.

ordinal variable | a numeric or character categorical variable in which the categories are ordered, but the category values convey no additional information beyond membership and order. In particular, the number of levels between two categories is not informative, and for numeric variables, the difference between category values is not informative. The results of an analysis that includes ordinal variables will typically be unchanged if you replace all the values of an ordinal variable by different numeric or character values as long as the order is maintained, although some algorithms may use the numeric values for initialization.

outlier   a data item whose value falls outside the bounds enclosing most of the other corresponding values in the sample. May indicate anomalous data. Outliers should be examined carefully; they may carry important information.

output   a variable computed from the inputs as a prediction/guess of the value of the target variables Synonyms: predicted value, estimate, y-hat.

parallel processing   the coordinated use of multiple processors to perform computational tasks. Parallel processing can occur on a multiprocessor computer or on a network of workstations or PCs.

parameter   the true or optimal value of the weights or other quantities (such as standard deviations) in a model.

partitioning   the act of breaking up a set of field values into discrete groups based on similarity with respect to a dependent variable as determined by a test of statistical significance.

pattern   a set of relationships between fields of data typically derived through statistical methods as in predictive modeling. Typically, the emphasis is on the display of the pattern as opposed to the prediction.

PMML   Predictive Modeling Markup Language. PMML describes data mining models in the Extensible Markup Language (XML), a universal format to describe structured documents and data designed by W3C group (http://www.w3c.org). The format was designed by (http://www.dmg.org) and enables researchers and commercial users to carry out various data mining tasks in a universal notation that is shared across

	environments. Typically, these environments employ proprietary standards that would otherwise make interoperation difficult, if not impossible.
population	the set of all cases that you want to be able to generalize to. The data to be analyzed in data mining are usually a subset of the population.
predictive model	a model with a target or outcome field or variable that is shown to be a function of one or more input or predictor fields or variables. Outcomes may be categorical (buy/no buy) or continuous (dollars spent; time spent). With categorical outcomes the models are called classification models, and with continuous outcomes they are called regression models.
prospective data analysis	a process that predicts future trends, behaviors, or events based on historical data.
qualitative	a process or entity that is defined in qualitative or non-exacting forms of measurement.
quantitative	a process or entity that is defined in quantitative, numerically based terms.
random forest	a collection of multiple decision trees that produce an average estimate for the target. In each node, a branch search is made on a random set of inputs instead of the full set of inputs. Each decision tree in the random forest is grown on a bootstrap sample of the training data set.
ratio variable	a numeric variable for which ratios of values are informative. In SAS Enterprise Miner, ratio and higher-level variables are not generally distinguished from interval variables, since the analytical methods are the same. However, ratio measurements are required for some computations in model assessment, such as profit and ROI measures.

record	a piece of information contained in a database that comprises an entry for each field in the database. For example, an employee database contains a record for each employee.
retrospective data analysis	a process that provides insights into trends, behaviors, or events that have already occurred.
root node	the node at the very top of a hierarchical decision tree display. In this node, values in the dependent variable are also represented.
row	the second dimension—along with column—of a traditional table. Since data sets are usually stored in tables, then the observations, or examples, that are captured by the data set are considered to be rows.
rule induction	the extraction of useful if-then rules from data that is based on statistical significance.
sample	a subset of the population that is available for analysis.
scoring	a method of applying a trained model to data to compute outputs. Synonyms: running (for neural nets), simulating (for neural nets), filtering (for decision trees), interpolating or extrapolating.
signal	a predictable variation in a target variable. It is often assumed that target values are the sum of signal and noise, where the signal is a function of the input variables. Synonyms: function, systematic component.
significance	a measure of the strength of a relationship between sample elements based on statistical probability.
split	a partition in a set of field values.
standard deviation	the square root of the variance. It is the measure of the level of variability in a collection of data. The larger the number, the greater the variability.
stochastic gradient boosting	see boosting.

subtree	a subset of the full decision tree created by pruning one or more branches up from the bottom of the tree. Subtrees always contain the root node.
supervised learning	an environment where the goal is to predict or classify the value of an outcome or target measure based on a number of input measures.
surrogate	the use of the predictive information that is held in a field, which is closely associated with the field that is being used as an input to form a branch. For example, if a value is missing for an input, then a surrogate may be used to estimate the likely value of the input at that point in the decision tree.
target	a field or variable that is being examined, estimated estimated, or described with the data mining model or process. It is synonymous with a dependent variable in a statistical analysis or a modeled outcome. The target variable value is known in some currently available data, but will be unknown in some future/fresh/operational data set. You want to be able to predict/guess the values of the target variables from other known variables. Synonyms: dependent variable, response, observed values, training values, desired output, correct output, outcome.
test data	a type of data that contains input and target values, not generally used during model training, but instead used to estimate generalization error. Test data is designed to provide an estimate of model performance in novel situations, and is ideally an independent collection of data that is separate from the data used in training the model.
time series analysis	the analysis of a sequence of measurements made at specified time intervals. Time is usually the dominating dimension of the data.

trained model	a specific formula or algorithm for computing outputs from inputs, with all weights or parameter estimates in the model chosen via a training algorithm from a class of such formulas or algorithms designated by the model. Synonym: fitted model.
training	the process of computing good values for the weights in a model, or, for tree-based models, choosing good split variables and split values. Synonyms: estimation, fitting, learning, adaptation, induction, growing trees.
training data	a type of data that contains input and target values used for training to estimate weights or other parameters. This is the data that is used to develop the data mining model. The notion of training derives from a machine-learning approach whereby the underlying development model mimics the extraction of knowledge from data through the use of lines of data as training instances.
twoing	a node partitioning technique that segments the classes in a node into two groups by combining classes together that form up to 50 percent of the data.
unsupervised learning	an environment where there is no outcome measure. The goal is to describe the associations and patterns among a set of input measures.
validation data	a type of data that contains input and target values used indirectly during training for branch selection and to determine when to form terminal nodes.
variable	an item of information represented in numeric or character form for each case in a data set. Both targets and inputs are variables. Synonyms: column, feature, attribute, coordinate, measurement.

variance

a measure of the range of values in a distribution that also combines a measure of the density. Sometimes referred to as the second moment around the mean. The expected value of the square of the deviations of a random variable from its mean value.

weight

a numeric value used in a model that is usually unknown or unspecified prior to the analysis. Weights may be estimated by the model or may be used in computing model results. Synonyms: estimated parameters, estimates, coefficients, betas.

References

Alexander, W. P., and S. D. Grimshaw. 1996. "Treed Regression." *Journal of Computational and Graphical Statistics* 5:156-175.

Amit, Y., and D. Geman. 1997. "Shape Quantization and Recognition with Randomized Trees." *Neural Computation* 9, no. 7:1545-1588.

Barlow, T., and P. Neville. 2001. "A Comparison of 2-D Visualizations of Hierarchies." *Proceedings of the IEEE Symposium on Information Visualization 2001 (INFOVIS'01).* San Diego, CA: IEEE Computer Society.

Belsley, D. A., E. Kuh, and R. E. Welsch. 1980. *Regression Diagnostics.* New York, NY: John Wiley & Sons, Inc.

Belson, W. A. 1956. "A Technique for Studying the Effects of Television Broadcast." *Applied Statistics* 5, no. 3:195-202.

Biggs, D., B. de Ville, and E. Suen. 1991. "A Method of Choosing Multiway Partitions for Classification and Decision Trees." *Journal of Applied Statistics* 18, no. 1:49-62.

Blyth, C. R. 1972. "On Simpson's Paradox and the Sure-Thing Principle." *Journal of the American Statistical Association* 67, no. 338:364-366.

Breiman, L. 1996. "Bagging Predictors." *Machine Learning* 24, no. 2:123-140.

Breiman, L. 2001. "Random Forests." *Machine Learning* 45, no. 1:5-32.

Breiman, L. 2002. "WALD Lectures." Paper presented at the sixty-fifth annual meeting of the Institute of Mathematical Statistics, Banff, Alberta, Canada. Available at http://www.stat.berkeley.edu/users/breiman/.

Breiman, L., et al. 1984. *Classification and Regression Trees.* Belmont, CA: Wadsworth.

de Ville, B. 1990. "Applying Statistical Knowledge to Database Analysis and Knowledge Base Construction." *Proceedings of the Sixth IEEE Conference on Artificial Intelligence Applications.* Seattle, Washington: IEEE Computer Society. 30-36

Doyle, P. 1973. "The Use of Automatic Interaction Detector and Similar Search Procedures." *Operational Research Quarterly* 24:465-467.

Doyle, P., and I. Fenwick. 1975. "The Pitfalls of AID Analysis." *Journal of Marketing Research* 12:408-413.

Einhorn, H. J. 1972. "Alchemy in the Behavioral Sciences." *Public Opinion Quarterly* 36:367-378.

Fisher, R. A. 1936. "The Use of Multiple Measurements in Taxonomic Problems." *Annals of Eugenics*. No. 7. Part II: 179-188.

Freund, Y. and R. E. Schapire. 1996. "Experiments with a New Boosting Algorithm." *Proceedings of the Thirteenth International Conference on Machine Learning*. Bari, Italy. 148-156.

Freund, Y. and R. E. Schapire. 2000. "Discussion of Additive Logistic Regression: A Statistical View of Boosting." *Annals of Statistics*. 28:391-393.

Friedman, H. J. 1999. "Greedy Function Approximation: A Gradient Boosting Machine." *The Annals of Statistics* 29, no. 5:1189-1232. Available at http://stat.stanford.edu/~jhf/ftp/trebst.ps.

Friedman, H. J., T. Hastie, and R. Tibshirni. 2000a. "Additive Logistic Regression: A Statistical View of Boosting." *Annals of Statistics*. 28:337-374.

Friedman, H. J., T. Hastie, and R. Tibshirni. 2000b. "Rejoiner for Additive Logistic Regression: A Statistical View of Boosting." *Annals of Statistics*. 28:400-407.

Green, D. M. and J. A. Swets. 1966. *Signal Detection Theory and Psychophysics*. New York: NY. John Wiley & Sons, Inc.

Hastie, T., R. Tibshirani, and J. Friedman. 2001. *The Elements of Statistical Learning: Data Mining, Inference, and Prediction*. New York, NY: Springer-Verlag.

Hawkins, D. M., and G. V. Kass. 1982. "Automatic Interaction Detection." In *Topics in Applied Multivariate Analysis*, ed. D. M. Hawkins. Cambridge: Cambridge University Press.

Ho, T. B., et al. 2002. "Mining from Medical Data: Case Studies in Meningitis and Stomach Cancer Domains." *Sixth International Conference on Knowledge-based Intelligent Information and Engineering Systems*. Crema, Italy. 547-551.

Hunt, E., J. Marin, and P. Stone. 1966. *Experiments in Induction*. New York, NY: Academic Press.

Kahneman, D., P. Slovic, and A. Tversky, eds. 1982. *Judgment under Uncertainty: Heuristics and Biases*. New York: Cambridge University Press.

Kass, G. V. 1975. "Significance Testing in Automatic Interaction Detection." *Applied Statistics* 24, no. 2:178-189.

Kass, G. V. 1980. "An Exploratory Technique for Investigating Large Quantities of Categorical Data." *Applied Statistics* 29, no. 2:119-127.

Lazarsfeld, P. F., and M. Rosenberg. 1955. *The Language of Social Research: A Reader in the Methodology of Social Research.* Glencoe, IL: The Free Press.

Loh, W. Y., and N. Vanichsetakul. 1988. "Tree-Structured Classification via Generalized Discriminant Analysis." *Journal of the American Statistical Association* 83:715-728.

Loh, W. Y., and Y. S. Shih. 1997. "Split Selection Methods for Classification Trees." *Statistica Sinica* 7:815-840.

McKenzie, D. P., et al. 1993. "Constructing a Minimal Diagnostic Decision Tree." *Methods of Information in Medicine* 32, no. 2:161-166.

Meyers, Y. 1990. "Ondelettes et opérateurs. I, Actualités Mathématiques [Current Mathematical Topics]." Herman. Paris

Michie, D. 1991. "Methodologies from Machine Learning in Data Analysis and Software." *The Computer Journal* 34, no. 6:559-565.

Michie, D., and Claude Sammut. 1991. "Controlling a Black-Box Simulation of a Spacecraft." *AI Magazine* 12, no. 1:56-63.

Michie, D., C. C. Spiegelhalter, and C. C. Taylor, eds. 1994. *Machine Learning, Neural and Statistical Classification,* New York, NY: Ellis Horwood

Miller, George A. 1956. "The Magical Number Seven, Plus or Minus Two: Some Limits on Our Capacity for Processing Information." *Psychological Review* 63:81-97.

Morgan, J. N., and J. A. Sonquist. 1963. "Problems in the Analysis of Survey Data, and a Proposal." *Journal of the American Statistical Association* 58:415-434.

Neville, P. 1999. "Growing Trees for Stratified Modeling." *Computing Science and Statistics* 30:528-533.

Pyle, Dorian. 1999. *Data Preparation for Data Mining.* San Francisco, CA: Morgan Kaufmann Publishers Inc.

Quinlan, J. R. 1979. "Discovering Rules by Induction from Large Collections of Examples." In *Expert Systems in the Micro-Electronic Age*, ed. D. Michie, 168-201. Edinburgh: Edinburgh University Press.

Quinlan, J. R. 1987. "Simplifying Decision Trees." *International Journal of Man-Machine Studies*. 27: 221-234.

Quinlan, J. R. 1993. *C4.5: Programs for Machine Learning*. San Francisco, CA: Morgan Kaufmann Publishers Inc.

Reddy, R. K. T., and G. F. Bonham-Carter. 1991. "A Decision-Tree Approach to Mineral Potential Mapping in Snow Lake Area, Manitoba." *Canadian Journal of Remote Sensing* 17, no. 2:191-200.

Shapiro, A. D. 1987. *Structured Induction in Expert Systems*. Wokingham, UK: Addison-Wesley.

Sonquist, J. A., E. Baker, and J. Morgan. 1973. *Searching for Structure (ALIAS-AID-III)*. Ann Arbor, Michigan: Survey Research Center, Institute for Social Research, The University of Michigan.

Surowiecki, James. 2004. *The Wisdom of Crowds: Why the Many Are Smarter Than the Few and How Collective Wisdom Shapes Business, Economies, Societies and Nations*. New York, NY: Doubleday.

Weaver, W. and C. E. Shannon. 1949. *The Mathematical Theory of Communication*. Urbana, IL: University of Illinois Press. Republished in paperback 1963.

Weisberg, Herbert F., Jon A. Krosnick, and Bruce D. Bowen. 1989. *An Introduction to Survey Research and Data Analysis*. 2d ed. Glenview, IL: Scott Foresman.

Weiss, S. M., and C. A. Kulikowski. 1991. *Computer Systems That Learn: Classification and Prediction Methods from Statistics, Neural Nets, Machine Learning, and Expert Systems*. San Mateo, CA: Morgan Kaufmann Publishers Inc.

Index

Books Available from SAS® Press

support.sas.com/pubs

A Handbook of Statistical Analyses Using SAS®, Second Edition
by **B.S. Everitt**
and **G. Der**

Health Care Data and SAS®
by **Marge Scerbo, Craig Dickstein,**
and **Alan Wilson**

The How-To Book for SAS/GRAPH® Software
by **Thomas Miron**

In the Know... SAS® Tips and Techniques From Around the Globe
by **Phil Mason**

Instant ODS: Style Templates for the Output Delivery System
by **Bernadette Johnson**

Integrating Results through Meta-Analytic Review Using SAS® Software
by **Morgan C. Wang**
and **Brad J. Bushman**

Learning SAS® in the Computer Lab, Second Edition
by **Rebecca J. Elliott**

The Little SAS® Book: A Primer
by **Lora D. Delwiche**
and **Susan J. Slaughter**

The Little SAS® Book: A Primer, Second Edition
by **Lora D. Delwiche**
and **Susan J. Slaughter**
(updated to include SAS 7 features)

The Little SAS® Book: A Primer, Third Edition
by **Lora D. Delwiche**
and **Susan J. Slaughter**
(updated to include SAS 9.1 features)

The Little SAS® Book for Enterprise Guide® 3.0
by **Susan J. Slaughter**
and **Lora D. Delwiche**

The Little SAS® Book for Enterprise Guide® 4.1
by **Susan J. Slaughter**
and **Lora D. Delwiche**

Logistic Regression Using the SAS® System: Theory and Application
by **Paul D. Allison**

Longitudinal Data and SAS®: A Programmer's Guide
by **Ron Cody**

Maps Made Easy Using SAS®
by **Mike Zdeb**

Models for Discrete Date
by **Daniel Zelterman**

Multiple Comparisons and Multiple Tests Using SAS® Text and Workbook Set
(books in this set also sold separately)
by **Peter H. Westfall, Randall D. Tobias, Dror Rom, Russell D. Wolfinger,**
and **Yosef Hochberg**

Multiple-Plot Displays: Simplified with Macros
by **Perry Watts**

Multivariate Data Reduction and Discrimination with SAS® Software
by **Ravindra Khattree**
and **Dayanand N. Naik**

Output Delivery System: The Basics
by **Lauren E. Haworth**

Painless Windows: A Handbook for SAS® Users, Third Edition
by **Jodie Gilmore**
(updated to include SAS 8 and SAS 9.1 features)

The Power of PROC FORMAT
by **Jonas V. Bilenas**

PROC SQL: Beyond the Basics Using SAS®
by **Kirk Paul Lafler**

PROC TABULATE by Example
by **Lauren E. Haworth**

Professional SAS® Programmer's Pocket Reference, Fifth Edition
by **Rick Aster**

support.sas.com/pubs

Professional SAS® Programming Shortcuts, Second Edition
by **Rick Aster**

Quick Results with SAS/GRAPH® Software
by **Arthur L. Carpenter**
and **Charles E. Shipp**

Quick Results with the Output Delivery System
by **Sunil Gupta**

Reading External Data Files Using SAS®: Examples Handbook
by **Michele M. Burlew**

Regression and ANOVA: An Integrated Approach Using SAS® Software
by **Keith E. Muller**
and **Bethel A. Fetterman**

SAS® for Forecasting Time Series, Second Edition
by **John C. Brocklebank**
and **David A. Dickey**

SAS® for Linear Models, Fourth Edition
by **Ramon C. Littell, Walter W. Stroup,**
and **Rudolf Freund**

SAS® for Mixed Models, Second Edition
by **Ramon C. Littell, George A. Milliken, Walter W. Stroup,** and **Russell D. Wolfinger**

SAS® for Monte Carlo Studies: A Guide for Quantitative Researchers
by **Xitao Fan, Ákos Felsővályi, Stephen A. Sivo,**
and **Sean C. Keenan**

SAS® Functions by Example
by **Ron Cody**

SAS® Guide to Report Writing, Second Edition
by **Michele M. Burlew**

SAS® Macro Programming Made Easy
by **Michele M. Burlew**

SAS® Programming by Example
by **Ron Cody**
and **Ray Pass**

SAS® Programming for Researchers and Social Scientists, Second Edition
by **Paul E. Spector**

SAS® Programming in the Pharmaceutical Industry
by **Jack Shostak**

SAS® Survival Analysis Techniques for Medical Research, Second Edition
by **Alan B. Cantor**

SAS® System for Elementary Statistical Analysis, Second Edition
by **Sandra D. Schlotzhauer**
and **Ramon C. Littell**

SAS® System for Regression, Third Edition
by **Rudolf J. Freund**
and **Ramon C. Littell**

SAS® System for Statistical Graphics, First Edition
by **Michael Friendly**

The SAS® Workbook and *Solutions* Set
(books in this set also sold separately)
by **Ron Cody**

Selecting Statistical Techniques for Social Science Data: A Guide for SAS® Users
by **Frank M. Andrews, Laura Klem, Patrick M. O'Malley, Willard L. Rodgers, Kathleen B. Welch,**
and **Terrence N. Davidson**

Statistical Quality Control Using the SAS® System
by **Dennis W. King**

A Step-by-Step Approach to Using the SAS® System for Factor Analysis and Structural Equation Modeling
by **Larry Hatcher**

A Step-by-Step Approach to Using SAS® for Univariate and Multivariate Statistics, Second Edition
by **Norm O'Rourke, Larry Hatcher,**
and **Edward J. Stepanski**

Step-by-Step Basic Statistics Using SAS®: Student Guide and *Exercises*
(books in this set also sold separately)
by **Larry Hatcher**

support.sas.com/pubs

Survival Analysis Using SAS®:
A Practical Guide
by **Paul D. Allison**

Tuning SAS® Applications in the OS/390 and z/OS
Environments, Second Edition
by **Michael A. Raithel**

Univariate and Multivariate General Linear Models:
Theory and Applications Using SAS® Software
by **Neil H. Timm**
and **Tammy A. Mieczkowski**

Using SAS® in Financial Research
by **Ekkehart Boehmer, John Paul Broussard,**
and **Juha-Pekka Kallunki**

Using the SAS® Windowing Environment:
A Quick Tutorial
by **Larry Hatcher**

Visualizing Categorical Data
by **Michael Friendly**

Web Development with SAS® by Example, Second Edition
by **Frederick E. Pratter**

Your Guide to Survey Research Using the
SAS® System
by **Archer Gravely**

JMP® Books

JMP® for Basic Univariate and Multivariate Statistics:
A Step-by-Step Guide
by **Ann Lehman, Norm O'Rourke, Larry Hatcher,**
and **Edward J. Stepanski**

JMP® Start Statistics, Third Edition
by **John Sall, Ann Lehman,**
and **Lee Creighton**

Regression Using JMP®
by **Rudolf J. Freund, Ramon C. Littell,**
and **Lee Creighton**

support.sas.com/pubs